T0287036

The Mystics Would Like a Word

THE

MYSTICS
Would Like a Word

*Six Women Who Met God
and Found a Spirituality for Today*

SHANNON K. EVANS

CONVERGENT
New York

ISBN 9780593727270
Ebook ISBN 9780593727287

Printed in the United States of America on acid-free paper

convergentbooks.com

2 4 6 8 9 7 5 3 1

First Edition

Book design by Fritz Metsch

For every woman whose story
merited an examination it never received

Contents

THÉRÈSE OF LISIEUX

CATHERINE OF SIENA

In a voiced community, we all flourish.

—TERRY TEMPEST WILLIAMS, *When Women Were Birds*

Introduction

This book is a sheer accident—that is, if you believe in such things, which I'm not sure I do. History has never been my strong suit and, as far as my faith goes, medieval saints never carried much weight with me. I used to prefer my spiritual heroes more modern, more relatable. Give me the Dorothy Days, the Óscar Romeros, the Thomas Mertons. Give me the writings that don't put me straight to sleep.

When I first became Catholic a decade ago, I was particularly frustrated by the female saints who were offered to me as role models. These women were always presented as docile and meek, women who could teach me about speaking in humility but not about speaking truth to power. There were exceptions, of course: I knew Catherine of Siena and Teresa of Ávila had spicy reputations, but no one really talked about why. Joan of Arc stood out as shockingly different, but the pacifist in me struggled with complicated feelings about her violent role in history. Mostly, I was content to let the study of saints be other people's thing and not my own.

But fate took a turn when a copy of Mirabai Starr's *Wild Mercy: Living the Fierce and Tender Wisdom of the Women Mystics* landed on my doorstep. At the time, I was freshly waking to a desire for a representation of the Divine feminine in my spiritual experience, so the premise of the book alone was enough to earn a click from my itchy online-ordering finger. Through Starr's work I was introduced to women mystics from many different religious traditions and spiritualities. At the time I wasn't even sure if I wanted to remain Christian, so I appreciated the wide scope. And yet, a bit to my surprise, the Christian mystics she pointed to were my favorites. The women I assumed I knew best surprised me the most. I found that when their thoughts were translated for me by a female (and an ethnically Jewish one, free from obligatory deference to Christian institutions and authorities, at that), these women became real, fascinating, layered, and, well, believable. It made me realize that the traditional presentation of the female saints and mystics had been funneled through and crafted for the male gaze. What's more, I realized that in my snobbery of assuming they had nothing to teach me, I was complicit in our collective reduction of who these women were and what they had to say.

The deal was sealed about a year later when I came across a quotation from a papal nuncio (a regional representative of the pope) about Teresa of Ávila during her lifetime. Good ol' Archbishop Filippo Sega said, "She is a restless gadabout, a disobedient and contumacious woman who invented wicked doctrines and devotions, and . . . has gone about to teach others in contradiction to the teaching of St. Paul who had forbidden women to teach."

Well, all right then, sister. I'll follow your ass off a cliff.

And so began my spiritual love affair with these women. First Teresa, then Julian of Norwich, then Hildegard of Bingen, Margery Kempe, Catherine of Siena, and finally, after some resistance, Thérèse of Lisieux. Each time I found the writings of another one, I would declare her my new favorite. I still can't pick. Because these women are the furthest thing from one-dimensional, despite how they have been portrayed. They are not irrelevant or demurring, nor are they fragile. (Okay, Thérèse of Lisieux might be a bit demurring and fragile, but you'll see why she earns her spot in this book.) These are women who are self-determining, stubborn, opinionated, gutsy, and unapologetically themselves. Five out of the six featured in this book were nuns, and despite my earliest prejudices, their vocation was not because they were docile but precisely because they *weren't*. I learned that convents were historically life rafts for women who eschewed the dutiful existence of marriage and motherhood—not to mention the high probability of death through childbirth. In the convent, a woman could retain her agency and bodily autonomy. She could devote herself to her theological passions. Often, she could receive an education. It is no coincidence that some of the strongest female voices in history have been those of professed religious sisters, which is still true in the Catholic Church today. The only lay-woman in this book is Margery Kempe, a mother of fourteen who wrestled mightily with the tension between her vocation as wife and mother and her spiritual calling to prayer and teaching.

The word *mystic* has an otherworldly quality about it; we tend to associate it with hermits levitating on a hillside more than with regular people living pretty regular lives—much less with ourselves. But a mystic is really just someone who has experienced a glimpse of the eternal and has chosen to pursue more. Mysticism is not reserved for a select few but is an invitation extended to each of us. Only one lifetime ago, the Jesuit theologian Karl Rahner said, "The Christian of the future will either be a mystic or will not exist." For many of us, that choice feels eerily personal.

Luckily, we have not been left without guides. The six women in these pages are more than able to lead us: they had great minds and fervent longings and have not been given adequate credit for their contributions to humankind's spiritual progress across time, geography, and religion. Which brings us back to why this book accidentally exists.

Once I discovered the treasure trove that is the wisdom of the female mystics, I came to see how relevant their insights continue to be for us today. I found myself shocked at how progressive their musings were and how timely they feel at this particular moment in history. Can we refer to God in the feminine? Ask Julian of Norwich. How does mental illness inform our spiritual experience? Margery Kempe would like a word. Should we keep politics out of church? Catherine of Siena has thoughts.

When I told my theologian friend Ellie that I was writing this book, she said she sees the female mystics as ambassadors for Christianity. For those who avoid our religion for fear of its most radical iterations, their expansive theologies carve out rooms of welcome for the seeker. And for those of us who find ourselves on the margins of our own Church, unsure of whether or not we want to jump ship, the women in this book make us believe it's possible to stay.

One of the things I find most compelling about Christianity—and a big reason why I stick around, despite frequent disillusionment—is its width. The depth matters, too, of course, but in my observation, depth can be found in any or no religion, if one is committed to finding it. But it is the wideness of Christianity that both challenges and affirms me; the fact that such very different kinds of people could find a home under the same spiritual tent. James Joyce once famously said of the Catholic Church, "Here comes everybody." Even if you're not Catholic, it's fair to say that Joyce's assessment stands for all of us. If you identify as Christian, no matter your bent, I'd be willing to bet that you have often found yourself categorized with people who drive you nuts. And in the age of such globalism, such pluralism, it is easier than ever to simply walk away; it's justifiable, even, given what we know now about the prevalence of abuse in our churches and the ways our missionary efforts advanced colonialism. Many people I love have ceased to identify as Christian, and I don't fault them for it. I understand the trauma, grief, and disillusionment that led them out.

And yet, I am still here. I value my religious tradition; its language, symbols, rituals, and culture are the portals that have taken me into an experience of God since I was a child, and I do not desire to leave them behind. So I've resolved to keep on digging the well of Christianity until I strike living water—again, and again, and again. But I have found this to be an impossible task without the companionship of like-minded friends, both living and dead.

The six women in these pages are some of those friends, and my dearest hope is that they might become yours as well. As interest in feminine spirituality is piqued around the world, we would be remiss to ignore (or worse, water down) the guides we've already been given. We don't have to reinvent the wheel. There is a reason the writings of these women have stood the test of time and reverberated across centuries. May we honor them as ancestors. May we have the maturity to recognize the timelessness of their wisdom, even as we build on and expand it so many years later.

A few words about the content of this book are in order before you dive in. It pains me that there are no Blacks, Indigenous folks, or People of Color represented among these six mystics. Part of wrestling with the cold, hard truth of Christianity is that its historical mixing with European political power resulted in the near-total erasure of certain voices. White, middle- to upper-class narratives are the ones our particular religious tradition has preserved, much to its grievous detriment.

I applied a list of criteria when deciding which women to include in these pages; I chose universally recognized female Christian mystics who had written at least one book for me to study and cite. While the Catholic Church has canonized multitudes of saints of all ethnicities from around the world, most did not write extensively, and little is known about their inner lives. Countless other women are deserving of the title of mystic beyond those included here, but these six are the ones who rose to the top.

I also want to acknowledge that each of these women was writing in a specific time and place in human history—and history has shown us how harmful some of their assumptions and attitudes were. I won't quote ideas I find repugnant in this book, but if you dig further into their works, you will find instances of anti-Semitism, xenophobia, misogyny, toxic asceticism, and more. While this is disappointing coming from our spiritual mentors, it gives us an opportunity to reflect on the privilege we have of living at this point in the evolution of human consciousness, perhaps especially as it relates to our view of God. Please also note that in Chapter 4 I address Margery Kempe's history as a victim of marital rape because I find it a hugely important and almost entirely undiscussed part of her story. If this is a triggering topic for you, please take care of yourself while reading this section, or choose to skip it if necessary.

Finally, I want to be clear that I am not a historian and, while heavily researched, this book is not an academic undertaking. Rather, my goal in these pages is spiritual: I hope this book enriches your contemplative prayer life, gives you permission to be curious and even change your mind, and rejuvenates your relationship with God. If it propels you to read the works of the mystics for yourself, I'd caution that translation matters, so choose wisely. You can never go wrong with Mirabai Starr.

So now may we position ourselves under the wise spiritual motherhood of these six mystics to grapple with questions of faith and liberation in our modern world, believing that the One Who Is Divine Mystery will remain large enough to hold us all most lovingly under Their tent.

TERESA OF ÁVILA

CHAPTER ONE

Trusting Yourself Doesn't Make You a Heretic

I read the words on the screen with a tightening in my chest. It wasn't uncommon for me to get criticism from fundamentalists on my Instagram, but their words were usually at least coated in something resembling civility. On this day one particular woman had come with claws out. "Stop pretending to be Christian," she rebuked me in the comments on my post. "You are purposefully deceiving people. It's obvious to all of us that you are Wiccan."

Spoiler alert: Gentle reader, I am not Wiccan. I don't think I even know any Wiccans. The extent of my familiarity with Wicca comes from the character Willow in the *Buffy the Vampire Slayer* television series that I watched as a teenager, which is to say, less than exhaustive but pretty witty.

And yet, in that moment, my heart raced and my cheeks burned as though I had been found out. I felt publicly exposed and vulnerable, not because I was being correctly outed as a pagan but because, as incorrect as her diagnosis was, this commenter had picked up on something true: I had transgressed the laws of Christian womanhood.

My crime? I had written a post that put language to the wild, raw, hungry spirits inside of women, the places in us that marvel at—and sometimes fear—the power of the mysteries within. The last sentence I wrote was "We will never be satisfied with a small God or a small inner flame. We know in our bodies there is more."

It was simple, this call to listen to and honor the deepest stirrings within. But the prospect of self-honesty, of attending to the desire to live untamed, terrified this woman. Her terror turned itself onto me, a conflict-averse person for whom that was difficult. But it wasn't about me at all. It was about her consciousness and her cages warring against each other. From behind the bars of patriarchy, women can be downright cruel to those who wander free.

This is an extreme example, of course. Most of us are not leaving hateful comments on other women's social media posts. (If you are . . . please stop.) For most of us, the battle is internal. Do we acknowledge the rumbling in our guts or do we continue reading from the script we've been given?

Too often, certain issues feel unwelcome in our faith spaces, while our faith might feel unwelcome in spaces of important social critique. When I say, for example, that I am Christian and feminist, I find the Christian part scares the feminists and the feminism part scares the Christians. Like many women today, I have felt pressured to choose between religious fidelity and progressive thinking. I have been there before—and I have no intention of going back.

A handful of years ago I was a much-lauded writer for a prominent Catholic women's ministry, where I enjoyed a sense of belonging and friendship. Community has always been an integral part of my spiritual life, and the women in this ministry were my primary community at the time; these were individuals with a spectrum of social, political, and theological beliefs but whose group identity leaned more conservative than my own. Still, I was convinced there was a place for me with them, especially since my writing was so well received. So I censored my more controversial opinions and convictions in order to fit in with the group. Worse, I performed serious mental gymnastics to lie to myself about being okay with some of the things said, done, and taught in the ministry. I didn't feel full permission to trust myself, my own conscience, or the way I understood the Spirit inside me, so I deferred to others instead.

Gradually, I began to wake up. Prompted by trials in my personal life that forced me to confront honestly the extent to which I had disconnected from my authentic self, I found the courage to return to my own instincts and voice. I employed small critiques of patriarchy in my writing and advocated for serious leadership positions, including ordination, for women in religious institutions. I criticized the blending of church and state for politicians' personal gain. I spoke openly about my love of yoga and the Enneagram. Even though I expressed these opinions only on my personal blog and social media accounts, my status within the ministry began to crumble. Complaints were lodged against me by longtime readers, which felt as humiliating as it was infuriating. A priest and a bishop worked to shut me up, which opened my eyes to the subtleties of clericalism's harm. When I was told by ministry leadership that I would be required to hide my personal convictions entirely if I wanted to stay on staff, I resigned in what I hoped would be a gracious and amicable fashion. To my shock, the vast majority of women I once counted as friends never spoke to me again. The feeling of having been used and then abandoned hurt more than the censorship.

The grief went deep. I lost friendships I had assumed were real. I lost my largest writing platform. I lost my spiritual community and sense of belonging. I mourned this all for months—and, if

I'm honest, a part of me still mourns it. And yet, I learned what
it felt like to be true to myself. I learned that I could trust myself.
It was more than worth it.

I know I am not alone in having gone through an experience
like this. When you consider how common these pressures are,
it's no wonder women are plagued by anxiety and depression.
For the sake of maintaining our sense of belonging, we discipline
ourselves into staying within the received boundaries of what we
are *allowed to* think, believe, or practice rather than what we *actually* think, believe, or want to practice. We look to spouses, family
members, pastors, and news anchors to tell us what parameters
we ought to stay within. We trust the authority of outside voices
far more than we trust the guidance of our own souls. In fact, the
very idea of trusting ourselves elicits unease: isn't that the very
thing the Bible tells us not to do?

It's true, there are places in the Bible that discourage us from
putting trust in ourselves. When I was a good Baptist kid growing
up in Bible Drill competitions, one of the first verses I memorized
was Proverbs 3:5–6: "Trust in the Lord with all your heart, and
do not rely on your own insight. In all your ways acknowledge
him, and he will make straight your paths" (NRSV). I'm not
saying this isn't wisdom: trusting in ourselves apart from our
union with God can indeed be a recipe for disaster. When we
are not attuned to our Life Source, we tend to be pretty selfish
and destructive people.

But that doesn't mean we throw away our inner compass. If we
are sincerely seeking to live in union with the Spirit, then trusting
in ourselves as portals of Divine life can be a way to move from
spiritual childhood into spiritual maturity. Jesus himself said the
kingdom of heaven is not to your left or to your right but is within
you (Luke 17:21). If we're honest, that's a frightening prospect.

It can feel safer to look for the kingdom of heaven outside of ourselves, to look for it in authority figures, religious culture, or the safety net of orthodoxy. There is a certain kind of felt security that comes with believing someone else knows more than we do, that somehow they have reached transcendent answers we are not even capable of touching. Jesus' words are all well and good, but when it comes down to it, we are more convinced that what he wants is for us to outsource our spiritual lives to a select few.

But what if, when Jesus said the kingdom of heaven is within you, what he meant was—and bear with me now—that the kingdom of heaven is within you? *I know. Crazy.* What if you actually do have a still, small voice to guide you? What if you actually do have everything you need for life and godliness? What if it's not a matter of being taught what to believe but a matter of being taught how to listen deeply to what you already do believe?

If you were taught to trust yourself, how might your experience of God be different? How might your entire existence be different? And if such a thing were possible, who would teach you?

*   *   *

Teresa of Ávila was born Teresa de Cepeda y Ahumada in 1515 in Spain. Her family lineage was Jewish, but rampant anti-Semitism and the force of the Christian empire compelled Teresa's paternal grandfather to convert to Catholicism in the hope of a better future for his children. But the family was sniffed out by the Spanish Inquisition for suspicion of practicing Judaism in their home. (In her book *Wild Mercy,* Mirabai Starr points out that since the matriarch of the family leads the sacred weekly Shabbat dinners, it is likely that Teresa's grandmother was the "guilty" party.) As punishment, the family was marched through the city streets for seven Fridays, clad in flamboyant costumes, and forced to kneel at every church and shrine while the townspeople jeered, spat, and threw stones. Had they not confessed, the punishment would have been far worse, perhaps even deadly.

Teresa's father was just a boy at this time and made an inner vow that neither he nor his own family would ever be subject to such public humiliation, becoming rigidly adherent to Catholic laws and customs. He got his wish, but not without close calls. For the latter half of her life, Teresa would be endlessly scrutinized and raked over by the Inquisition because of her ecstatic intimacy with God and her bold reformer's spirit—but I'm getting ahead of myself.

Teresa of Ávila was a handful right from the start. Imaginative and charming, intense and charismatic, she was a natural-born leader. As a child, she convinced her older brother to run away from home with her to evangelize the Moors and get beheaded so they could be martyrs. They made it as far as the city gates before getting caught and returned home. In her autobiography, Teresa admits that it wasn't love for God or the Moors that motivated her, but rather the attractiveness of getting to bypass Purgatory and make a postmortem beeline straight to the savory delights of heaven. When that plan failed, the children tried to become hermits instead, building cells out of small stones in the family orchard and becoming increasingly frustrated when the structures would topple over. Whatever you might say about Teresa, one thing you must admit: she was a human pulsing with vision.

Teresa's preteen and teen years, however, were marked by a shallowness that would later embarrass her. Heavily influenced by a friend and buoyed by the intrigue of her mother's romance novels, Teresa found herself caught up in gossip, vanity, and superficiality for several formative years, during which she also suffered the death of her beloved mother in childbirth. Then, somewhere around age sixteen, Teresa got caught in an indiscretion with a love interest. We don't have details, but this could have been anything from unsupervised conversation to premarital sex. The fallout was immediate: her scrupulous widower father sent Teresa to live at a convent for a short period as both consequence and protection. Yet to everyone's great surprise, including Teresa's, she thrived there. After a time of discernment, she entered a Carmelite monastery at nineteen and made her vows two years later, taking the name Teresa of Jesus.

Through the course of her consecrated life, Teresa wrote prolifically: she was a woman with something to say and the confidence to say it. Each of her four major works is considered invaluable to the evolution of the mystical tradition, but it is *The Interior Castle,* which she wrote near the end of her life, that is widely regarded as a spiritual masterpiece. In it she describes the soul as a castle with seven "dwellings" or "mansions" that spiral inward. The first mansion is the initial sincere step one takes toward God; the seventh is where a person experiences full unitive bliss with the Divine. And the five dwellings in between represent incremental stages of spiritual maturity and awakened consciousness along the journey. As we travel into spiritual maturity, she explains, we necessarily pass through each mansion of the interior castle, going deeper and deeper into ourselves—and all the while going deeper and deeper into God.

The radical posture of this idea can't be overstated, especially for a Spanish Catholic woman in the time of the Inquisition. Under the thumb of religious and political leaders hell-bent on retaining power, most people's spirituality consisted of deference to authority and fear of the afterlife. The ecclesiastical authorities took note of how radical Teresa's ideas were—and they tried to keep her from speaking. While Teresa had no desire to be rebellious for the sake of rebellion alone, she was also unapologetic about what she knew to be true. She stood steadfast before men with the power of the patriarchy behind them who were hoping to intimidate her into submission. Of them, she wrote, "I have had a great deal of experience with men of learning. I have also had experience with half-learned men who are full of fear and have cost me dearly."

Our girl can throw some shade.

Teresa taught that unity with God is not found by laboring up a ladder to get to heaven but rather by delving into the deepest mines within ourselves. Not an ascent, she would say, but a descent. This distinction is important. Many of us have spent years on the receiving end of religious messaging that told us we must transcend ourselves to be united with God; that can mean changing our personalities, not thinking for ourselves, suppressing our sexualities, obsessing over sin, or any number of other things. We all have unique stories, but often they boil down to the same thing: the message that you must rise above yourself to reach God, who is somewhere ambiguously *out there*. But Teresa calls bullshit.

Teresa tells us we don't have to rise above ourselves to encounter God but rather, with curiosity and vulnerability, we must dive within ourselves, further even than we thought we'd be comfortable going. "What could be worse than not being at home in our own house?" she asks. "What hope do we have of finding rest outside of ourselves if we cannot be at ease within?"

The interior castle spirals inward, with each "mansion" representing a more mature phase of spiritual development and life in God. As we learn to trust our own souls and count them worthy of attention and exploration, we begin to see that God is and has always been residing in them. And in the innermost chamber of our interior castle, Teresa says, our Beloved is waiting for us.

* * *

Like the prayer novice that I am, when I read *The Interior Castle* I spent a not insignificant amount of time trying to pinpoint exactly at which periods of my life I had gone through each mansion—and which mansion I might be in currently. It wasn't long before I found myself frustrated by the nebulous nature of this endeavor. Happily, I came across a story told by James Finley that recentered my reading.

Finley is a modern spiritual master in the Christian tradition. He is an expert in the study of the Spanish mystics Teresa of Ávila and John of the Cross, and he is one of the leading teachers of centering prayer. As a young man, he was mentored by Thomas Merton. Finley tells the story of being a mere eighteen years old and earnestly speculating to Merton about which of Teresa's seven mansions he was in at the time, hungrily asking his mentor for confirmation. Merton looked at him, shook his head, and said, "It's none of your damn business which one you're in!"

This story delights me to no end, and not just because I get tickled by holy people using words like *damn*. I love it because the story speaks to the universal human tendency to seek out any possible measurement to stack ourselves up against. We're always trying to assess whether we are ahead, behind, or incredibly average. We desperately seek some kind of metric to know whether we are on the right track, whether God is pleased with us, whether we should be feeling proud or ashamed.

It's garbage, isn't it? Merton knew that. Teresa would be horrified by her labor of love being leveraged as a pitiless measuring stick. But we who are still spiritually immature use it that way. We need the wise sages to remind us that it's none of our damn business how far along we are. It's only our business to carry on in love. This doesn't mean it's not helpful to assess our prayer practices or that anything is wrong with genuine longing to grow closer to experiential unity with God. But *The Interior Castle* is meant to expand our imaginations for what is possible in prayer and to help us feel less blind and alone as we journey. It's not meant to be a unit of comparison or metric of success.

It's the difference between approaching spirituality from a foundation of production and looking at it as a foundation of relationship. In the West, our religious structures almost always reflect our colonizing culture, where the victors are celebrated, competitiveness is a given, and progress is linear. Could we instead broaden our spiritual imaginations? With a foundation of relationship—with ourselves, with others, and with God— our faith can grow from a place of connection rather than from performing or conquering. In this more traditionally feminine approach, the health and wholeness of people take precedence over legalism and immovable absolutes. The life of Jesus is the embodiment of what it means to have a spiritual foundation of relationship. "The Sabbath was made for humans," he says, "not humans for the Sabbath." Spirituality is not a competition—not even against yourself.

If our faith formation is grounded in the nurture of relationship rather than the criticism inherent to projects of human accomplishment, then growth is framed and measured differently. In such an economy, failure is often the best teacher, solidarity trumps competition, and progress looks more like a spiral than a straight line.

In the past few years I have sought to make semiannual retreats a part of my life, and when I schedule them I always seek out a retreat center that has a labyrinth to walk. Following the slow, rhythmic lines of the spiral always seems to help me understand what the Spirit is doing inside me a bit better; I'm a sensory being, and I've found that embodied practices are the best at helping me process spiritual ideas.

The very first time I can remember walking a labyrinth was shortly after making my exit from the women's ministry I described earlier. Needless to say, I was an emotional mess: grieving and confused, yet hopeful and untethered. But more than anything, I was realizing how long I had actually been disconnected from my authentic interior life. Finding my way back home to myself was a daunting process.

At the Franciscan Renewal Center in Scottsdale, I tried my best to assume the meditative posture with which I imagined one should walk a labyrinth. But in truth I was flummoxed by what was going on beneath my feet, doubtful of how such nonsensical lines could ever lead me to the altar placed in the center. About halfway through the exercise, I panicked. *I did something wrong,* I thought, shoulders tensing up. *I should just hop over this line right here and go straight to the center. No one will see.*

Luckily, I caught on to the obvious spiritual parallel just in time to stop myself and to will my feet to keep following the path. I rounded the outer edge, seemingly as far as I could possibly be from the inside of the spiral, and suddenly, just a few steps later, there I was: right smack in the middle, invited to sit on the stone bench and survey my journey.

This, Teresa of Ávila would swear, is the spiritual life. Not a straight line, but a mass of winding steps that seem to take us far away from our goal, while our pilgrims' feet are pleading with us to trust the process. To trust ourselves. To trust the Spirit who leads us. There is no such thing as falling behind; there is no such thing as getting ahead; there is even no such thing as losing our way, for it is the Way who carries us.

*   *   *

"It is very important, friends, not to think of the soul as dark. We are conditioned to perceive only external light. We forget that there is such a thing as inner light, illuminating our soul."

If the words of Teresa of Ávila were groundbreaking in the Middle Ages, they somehow feel only marginally less so today, inundated as we are with the trademark Christian wariness of putting too much emphasis on the self. Our religious culture warns us of this through cherry-picked Scripture verses about *dying to self* and *binding up the flesh,* waving a blithe hand at passages about our already realized oneness with Christ. In these circles, one of the swiftest criticisms of modern spiritual books is that they "read like self-help books," as though spirituality and helping yourself could not possibly go hand in hand. Christian culture can be equally snide about phrases like *finding yourself* or *owning your truth,* believing that such self-exploration is for the immature and individualistic, not something we enlightened Christians need to do.

I wonder what such critics would do with Teresa of Ávila's thesis that the self is worthy of knowledge. Her writings center on the assumption that your self, your inner world, everything that is communicated in and through you, is holy and worthy of discovery. "What a shame that, through our own unconsciousness, we do not know ourselves!" she writes. "We rarely consider the soul's excellent qualities or who it is that dwells within her or how precious she really is. And so we don't bother to tend her beauty." Our problem, says Big Sis, is that "we don't understand the great secrets hidden inside of us."

Teresa of Ávila, one of history's masters of prayer, is convinced that we can't know God apart from knowing ourselves; that we move toward Divine union only when we seek to understand the secrets hidden within us and the sacred mysteries they contain. Seeing as how she is the internationally renowned mystical guru and we are not, maybe we should consider taking what she says seriously.

*   *   *

I've birthed a lot of babies. Four, to be exact, plus I'm mothering another one birthed by a woman who is co-parenting him from heaven. In my Catholic tradition, and in some other Christian denominations as well, one of the first questions a new mom is asked is "When are you getting the baby baptized?" Okay, Janet, I'm still bleeding from my hoo-ha and sleeping three hours a night here. Give it time.

There's a reason for this, and unfortunately, it's not just that Catholics jump on any excuse to throw a party (though that's also true). The urgency stems from the emphasis on original sin, the belief that the human soul is born inherently sinful and must be redeemed by baptism as quickly as possible. In light of this theology, Teresa of Ávila's urging to not view the soul as dark feels downright contradictory. When she reprimands us for forgetting about our inner light, I can't help but wonder how much more whole we would all be if the same message was preached in our churches.

I realize I'm stirring the pot here, but the emphasis on original sin has never resonated with me as a parent, nor was it ever what compelled me to see my infants baptized. My children's baptisms have been truly sacred experiences for me, some of the holiest days of my life. But being a mother has only deepened my conviction that the human soul is marked primarily by what some call "original blessing"—or, per Hildegard of Bingen, "original wisdom"—rather than original sin.

This does not deny our sinfulness, because its existence is quite obvious, but it shifts its emphasis to the backseat. Our belovedness and goodness are much more important, and also more reflective of our original identity in the biblical creation story. In fact, original sin is not a concept found at all in the Jewish Scriptures—in those writings that are said to be the foundation of the Christian faith and those that Jesus himself studied and quoted. The idea of original sin was first used in the fourth century by Saint Augustine, who might be surprised by how his ideas have grown. This isn't theological nit-picking. What we believe matters. How we view our most primal state determines how we feel about ourselves, our ability to accept God's love for us, and whether we feel permission to trust the Spirit within through our inner compass.

In his book *Original Blessing*, Episcopal priest and theologian Matthew Fox writes, "Whatever is said of original sin, it is far less hallowed and original than are love and desire, the Creator's for creation and our parents for one another. Our origin in the love of our parents and in their love-making, and the celebration of creation at our birth, are far, far more primeval and original in every sense of that word that is any doctrine of 'original sin.'"

This echoes loudly of the theology of Teresa of Ávila and her insistence on that inner light which illuminates our soul. Fox might call that inner light "original blessing." I might simply call it "Divine love." The words of Teresa I quoted at the beginning of this section call to mind those of the bride in Song of Songs. In the very first chapter the young lover says, "Dark am I, yet lovely." We don't have to pretend that our sin and weaknesses don't exist in order to embrace the light and loveliness of each of our souls. Resolving to trust in our souls does not mean we believe we are perfect. It is merely giving ourselves the dignity of trusting that when we mess up, when we fall short, when we "miss the mark" (as the word *sin* literally means), we will be able to recalibrate. The compass inside of us is strong and true, held fast by the One who holds all things together. We can be dark yet lovely. We can trust our inner light to guide us, because we trust that the reality of who we are is made up of much more than what we can see; the reality of who we are is that we exist in Divine union.

The soul is not something to make smaller so that, as some say, God can be made bigger within us. On the contrary, Teresa of Ávila encourages us to relish the vastness of the soul, to celebrate it as a sliver of God, a part of the fathomless expanse of love that is the great I AM. This can be trusted. *You* can be trusted.

Questions for Prayer and Reflection

1. Do you feel comfortable viewing your soul as a place of light? How has your answer been formed by external influences throughout your life?

2. Teresa of Ávila trusted herself and her own soul. What kind of inner response do you notice that her example evokes in you?

3. Have you given yourself permission to act upon your inner knowing, or do you defer to the advice or direction of others instead?

CHAPTER TWO

Sensuality, Sexuality, and Living
as a Person in a Body

The problem was sex, as the problem so often is. Oh, it might not have been intercourse. It might not even have been kissing or fondling. But sex is so much more than what actually happens between people; it's about an idea, a desire, a curiosity. Sex is about being alive.

So who knows what really happened when a young Teresa of Ávila was busted for an adolescent indiscretion? When writing about the event, she omits details with such precision that it's hard to determine if she's being modest or coy. Maybe the teens went to second base. Maybe they were just holding hands. Whatever happened that day, by Teresa's own account her fleshly desires were strong and passionate. "When I thought no one need ever know," she writes, "I risked many things which were both dishonorable and sins against God."

Piecing together the few details we are given, the gist of the matter is this: Teresa and a love interest did something together that was considered inappropriate. Whatever happened to the other party, if anything, we'll never know, but Teresa was sent by her father to a nearby Augustinian convent for eighteen months. The logic of this decision was twofold: a time of seclusion was unquestionably a form of consequence for a social butterfly such as Teresa, but it also functioned as a means of biding time for the community's collective memory to move on to the next piece of gossip. When she returned home, Teresa's father was already thinking about which well-established gentleman she should be given to in marriage. But, as we've seen, our girl had other plans.

Teresa explains, "I was still most anxious not to be a nun . . . though I was afraid of marriage also." Like so many women of the day, Teresa was forced to choose between two options that both felt unappealing. Ultimately, she describes choosing religious life because she thought it would keep her on the straight and narrow; but considering her mother's young death in childbirth, it's hard to believe that the loss of control over her own body— and, possibly, her own life—didn't play a part in her decision. Still, she clearly had a real calling to a life of devotion.

It was a far cry from the life that everyone had assumed she would live, as a beautiful and vivacious woman of means, but Teresa found that the life of an avowed religious suited her. She knew she didn't want to join the Augustinian community with whom she had lived; instead she followed a beloved nun friend to the Carmelite Convent of the Incarnation just outside the city of Ávila, where she professed her vows in 1536 at twenty-one years old.

The Carmelite house was a veritable buffet for young nuns: those who sought piety could be pious, those who sought frivolity could be frivolous. There was a smorgasbord of spiritualities and ways of living out vows, which is likely what attracted Teresa to the Carmelites instead of the Augustinians. It was also what likely led her to seek nationwide reforms of the order later in life, a movement for which she would become well-known.

But finding a home in the convent as a celibate didn't negate the fact that Teresa remained a traditionally sexual creature. Even after entering into religious life, she described how much she enjoyed flirting with the visitors who would come to the convent parlor every Friday to mingle with the sisters. Teresa would hold court then as she had in the past as a single young woman with suitors, all the while feeling conflicted and a little guilty for how much she enjoyed the attention. Teresa was hardwired for connection, and that hunger constantly sought satiation.

*   *   *

A few years ago my husband, Eric, and I met for several months with a fertility care practitioner who was helping us learn to chart my cycles and fertility signs in the hope of naturally avoiding pregnancy. She began our first session together with an explanation of human sexuality and how it is much broader than what we do in the sack; our sexual desires and activities also include emotional connection, physical touch, sensory input, sense of embodiment, grounded spiritual experiences, and more. "There are so many ways to connect sexually with each other that don't involve being naked!" she encouraged.

As someone who enjoys finding the interconnection between seemingly separate or dissimilar things, I liked this perspective. But as someone who, it turns out, also enjoys being naked, I wound up pregnant after a few meetings. Getting foot rubs on the couch just didn't have the same zing.

Even though my dalliance with this fertility practice was short-lived, the concept of a multifaceted and holistic view of sexuality stuck with me. Those familiar with the Enneagram will understand when I say I'm a nine, "the Peacemaker," which in my case means my default mode of existence is to forget I have a body at all. I am prone to blocking out or willfully ignoring every possible sign she could be giving me, so I like to try to keep an antenna up for tools or philosophies that can help me better pay attention. And the more I've carried this comprehensive view of sexuality around through the years, the more comfortable, confident, and integrated I have felt in my own body, both during and completely apart from sexual acts. (Don't clutch your pearls here: I have a basketball team's worth of children. Yes, I have sex and I like it.)

In her book *The Wisdom of Your Body,* psychologist Hillary McBride uses a model called the Five Circles of Sexuality, introduced by Dennis Dailey in the early 1980s, to illustrate a holistic concept of sexuality. The five circles, which overlap one another, are labeled intimacy, sexual health and reproduction, power and sexualization, sensuality, and sexual identity. Each one represents an important aspect of how we think and talk about sex, but not all have to do with intercourse itself. The reason this visual aid is helpful, McBride explains, is that we so often forget that "sexuality is not simply genital-to-genital contact but also the interpersonal expression of longings."

Neuroscientist and sex therapist Nan Wise adds, "We are all intrinsically sexual, we are always connecting, always communicating with others. Sex is bigger than genitals or body friction. . . . Being human, we are born to seek sexual connection; with the capacity to find pleasure with and through our connection with our bodies and with one another. Sex happens in the body and in the brain."

I find that in expansive discussions of sexuality like this one, especially as it relates to the spiritual life, it's helpful to highlight the sensuality circle in Dailey's model. *Sensuality* refers to the way we use our five senses to experience pleasure. Every human being, whether sexually active or not, has access to deep, embodied pleasure. Consider how good it feels to melt into a warm bath with scented salts at the end of a long, hard day. Or to savor the taste of a perfectly seasoned meal eaten on a patio on a cool summer's night. Or the way the right piece of music can elevate you to something like ecstasy. Such experiences are distinct but not separate from our sexuality. The circles overlap, remember? It's all about being a human fully alive in your body, relishing the pleasures she offers.

There is an endearing story about Teresa of Ávila that illustrates the need for sensuality. Over a gourmet partridge dinner that the revered nun was clearly enjoying, a friend of hers called the appropriateness of such a delicacy into question, given Teresa's holy reputation. "What would people think?" her friend asked with concern. Teresa shrugged, mouth full of meat. "Let them think what they want to think. There's a time for penance, and a time for partridge."

This account makes me smile every time I think of it, and it calls to mind the words of Jesus in Luke 7: "For John the Baptist has come eating no bread and drinking no wine, and you say, 'He has a demon,' the Son of Man has come eating and drinking, and you say, 'Look, a glutton and a drunkard, a friend of tax collectors and sinners!' Nevertheless, wisdom is vindicated by all her children" (NRSV). For all their different life experiences, Jesus and Teresa land at the exact same place. Haters gonna hate. You might as well suck the marrow out of life and trust that sneaky minx wisdom to vindicate her children.

If sensuality is sexuality, then sexuality is also spirituality. We are not meant to separate one from the other, even if various ones of us are called to live out our sexualities in different ways. It's incumbent upon each of us, whether sexually active like me or an avowed celibate like Teresa of Ávila, to integrate our sexuality in a healthy way. For if there's one thing we've learned by this point in history, it's that when we try to repress our sexuality in the name of spirituality, a whole host of toxins build up.

*   *   *

I never owned a purity ring, that effervescent midnineties symbol of abstaining from sex until marriage, but my big sister did. I'm not even sure exactly where she got the thing, because our parents and our home church all leaned pretty moderate. Our church actually boasted the first female Baptist pastor in Texas, and I can't imagine any pastor with a hyphenated last name thumbs-upping the delivery of purity rings to junior high girls. But however it came to her, Elise had one of those much-touted symbols of religious devotion at thirteen years old, long before she would be seriously confronted with big sexual decisions in the context of loving and equal relationships. Two years her junior, I can remember surveying the piece of jewelry on her hand with a mixture of awe and trepidation. It was clearly a "cool" thing to have if you were a Christian teenager at the time, but unlike my people-pleasing firstborn sister, I was never one to jump on any boat recommended to me by authority figures. I didn't own a purity ring, but I can't say I didn't absorb its moral code by osmosis.

My sister wasn't alone: it is now estimated that 2.5 million American teenagers had purity rings in the mid-1990s, and they remained a trend through the early 2000s, a fact that the Jonas Brothers will never live down. But even those of us who never donned the silver piece on our ring finger weren't immune to what it symbolized: the evangelical Christian obsession with sex, purity, and placing the onus of sexual responsibility on girls and women. You don't even have to be Christian to feel the impact of this perspective; like so many parts of our westernized

Christianity, it broadly affects our secular society in countless unconscious ways.

Still, the specific impact of this moral code has historically hit religious communities the hardest. Among those of us who are now removed from that worldview, it has come to be known as "purity culture." The associations that come with the term might differ among us depending on our unique experiences of spiritual communities, but Linda Kay Klein, author of the book *PURE: Inside the Evangelical Movement That Shamed a Generation of Young Women and How I Broke Free,* explains purity culture this way: "Everyone is expected to maintain absolute sexlessness before marriage (that means no sexual thoughts, feelings, or actions). . . . Men's thoughts and actions are said to be either pure or impure, while women themselves are said to be either pure or impure. . . . Purity culture also teaches that women are responsible for the sexual thoughts, feelings, and choices men make, and so must dress, walk, and talk in just the right way so as not to 'inspire' sexual thoughts, feelings, and actions in them. If they do 'inspire' such thoughts, they are said to be a 'stumbling block'—literally a thing over which men trip on their pathway to God."

Most people I know who were raised in Christian environments have had to do a lot of inner work to embrace their sexuality as something positive, sacred, and pleasurable. Many of us have had to wrestle to see our sexual desires and preferences as God-given. Youth pastors' sermons about lost virginity being akin to a wilted flower die hard—even if you played by their rules and saved that virginity for your marriage bed! After years of hearing messages about premarital sex being a character stain at best, or a moral evil at worst, it's nearly impossible for a person to flip the switch on their wedding night and suddenly feel perfectly comfortable gettin' it on with the one they love. Sadly, many of us are still trying to flip that switch decades later.

Even more dangerous, in our religious contexts most of us were conditioned to believe that anything other than heterosexual desires was grossly abnormal. Homophobia and transphobia run deep in purity culture. How many people have been conditioned to believe that their desires for intimacy make them dirty, unlovable, and repulsive to God when in reality a God of love rejoices in their hearts' longing to reflect Divine union? On top of that, because the architects of purity culture determined that the bodies of girls and women would have to bear the heavier burden of True Love Waits, the natural sexual awakening of girls was treated as threatening and filthy. Today we call this villainization of a woman's agency to determine her own sexual ethic "slut shaming," but back then it was just called "evangelicalism."

Add to this list of dynamics victim blaming and sexual repression and most of us have a whole heap of stuff that we are still working through in midlife. If you are not one of those people, consider yourself blessed indeed. The rest of us are still trying to figure this sex thing out.

But as we've established, your sexuality isn't limited to what happens between your sheets. A sexual ethic that finds its roots in fear and shame will bleed over into your other sensory experiences and your spiritual life, robbing you of the full vibrancy and aliveness that is your birthright as a creature made in the Divine image. Our bodies cannot be separated from our brains, or from our souls. Father Richard Rohr, a Franciscan friar and founder of the Center for Action and Contemplation in Albuquerque, has said, "If we are afraid of our sexuality, we are afraid of God."

Part of the task of growing in consciousness is learning to

integrate the physical with the spiritual. A faith that rejects false binaries is one that can put aside our old black-and-white thinking and tendency to compartmentalize, and embrace the shades of gray that form when the black and the white overlap.

If we insist on keeping spirituality and sexuality in their own respective boxes, we will stunt our growth in each. But if we open ourselves up to the possibility of integration, we find that a healthy sexuality (including nonerotic, sensory-based experiences) can deeply inform our spirituality, and vice versa. We see this process of maturity happen in Teresa of Ávila's account of her time in the Carmelite convent.

After taking vows of chastity as a young nun, Teresa at first struggled to figure out how to live her sexuality in ways that honored the boundaries she had drawn for herself. Flirting with visitors at the convent's weekly social night came naturally to her and met the longing for interpersonal connection that is at the heart of sexuality, but she felt an incongruence in herself afterward that she wasn't proud of. It took a while—how long, we aren't sure, but likely years—for Teresa to gradually lay to rest her empty flirtations as she began to experience sexual fulfillment through her spirituality instead.

If this sounds counterintuitive to you, consider these words from therapist Paul Giblin: "Sexuality and spirituality spring from the same vital life source and have the same end. They are both about relationship; loving and being loved, desiring and being desired; and being vulnerable, honest, and intimate. They both require growth in self-knowledge, including awareness of one's limitations and 'shadow.'" Hillary McBride adds, "Sexuality is not at odds with spirituality but, in fact, a deep human expression of it."

Along these lines, some of Teresa's descriptions of her spiritual experiences are downright racy. In the mystical tradition, the term *ecstasies* is used to describe full-body raptures in prayer that are physical and sensory as well as deeply transcendent. I probably don't need to point out to you that the word *ecstasy* can be interchanged with *orgasm,* and that, in fact, the descriptions of both often sound pretty similar. The same is true for the way mystics articulate union with the Divine; the similarities to sexual union just can't be denied. Listen to one description that Teresa offers from her own experience as an example: "In a state of union, the soul sees nothing and hears nothing and comprehends nothing. Union lasts such a short time, and it seems even shorter than it really is. God presses himself so fully against the inside of the soul that when she returns to herself the soul has no doubt whatsoever that God was in her and she was in God. This truth remains with her forever. Even though years may go by without God granting this blessing again, the soul can never forget. She never doubts: God was in her; she was in God."

Teresa, like many other mystics, frequently refers to union with God as a spiritual marriage between the Beloved and a person's soul. This spiritual marriage is "a coupling that will give birth to countless blessings," she promises her reader. With language like that, it's no wonder that the most famous depiction of Teresa in history, *Ecstasy of Saint Teresa,* a sculpture by Gian Lorenzo Bernini that sits in the Cornaro Chapel of the church of Santa Maria della Vittoria in Rome, depicts our girl looking like she's been caught mid-orgasm while an angel prepares to pierce her heart with a spear.

But not all of Teresa's most sensual metaphors were about, um, "coupling." She also exhibits her impressive level of comfort with human anatomy when she speaks of the soul being continuously sustained by streams of milk flowing from the Divine breasts; because, as she puts it, "It seems to be the will of the Beloved for these others to enjoy all that the spirit is enjoying." I mean, hell yeah. How does the saying go? Shared sorrow is half sorrow; shared joy is double joy. Let that holy breast milk flow.

And yet this holistic integration didn't end in Teresa's private life of prayer. A maturing Teresa also found a way to integrate her sexuality into her interpersonal relationships as she grew in care and closeness to the friends she held most dear. She, along with countless celibate people throughout history, learned to express her longing for connection through deeply committed friendship and a life of service. As she aged, Teresa took seriously the fact that the younger women in her convent looked to her as a mother, and she related to them with both fierce protectiveness and sensible embodiment. She found great meaning in her physicality within the Carmelite community; she tended the sick, washed the dishes, and consoled the desolate. Her sexuality found an outlet for human connection in community in ways most of us would never think to call sexual.

Author, theologian, and professor Elizabeth A. Dreyer notes the importance of friendship in Teresa's theological approach. Dreyer writes that Teresa "encouraged her readers to seek out others who practice prayer. She saw sharing conversation about the joys and trials of the spiritual life as a fitting way to nurture friendship with God. She knew the comfort of finding others who were also spiritually wounded and ill, but nevertheless willing to help each other." Through life in the convent, it would seem, Teresa learned what it was to have an embodied, relational faith.

Then, at fifty-two years old, Teresa met the man who would become her most intimate friend in life, a true soul mate in every sense of the word. John of the Cross was only twenty-five at the time and also a consecrated religious, so their relationship was never a physical one, at least not in the traditional sense of the word. But they alone spoke the language of each other's hearts and shared the rare gift of communing with God on a nearly untapped spiritual plane.

Teresa was animated, vivacious, and witty. John was quiet and gentle. They fit together like puzzle pieces and sharpened each other's theologies and language for the Divine. It is rumored that a fellow Carmelite sister once walked into the dining room where the two mystics had stayed up late talking into the night to find them both silently staring across the table at one another, each levitating a few inches off their respective chairs.

Did Teresa ever have intercourse with John? No. But if there was ever a relationship that illustrated the holistic nature of human sexuality, it was theirs: a resonance of supernatural connection in both body and soul.

*   *   *

If we are open to looking, we can find our own embodiment journey illustrated in Teresa's written account of her life. For someone who never set out to write about sex or sensuality, she sure has a lot to teach us about them. By sharing her story in a vulnerable and unselfconscious way, Teresa holds up a mirror to our own experiences, allowing us to make sense of them, and perhaps even to hope that body integration is still a possibility for us in our soul journey.

Teresa's life illustrates that in our youth, the natural human outworking of our sexuality is curiosity and experimentation. In our teens and twenties, maybe even our thirties, we are asking questions about what it means to be a person in a body and how our desires lead us to connection. It is awkward. It is confusing. We might have regrets. But this time of emergent sexuality is holy, and should be marked by wonder, not shame.

Not long ago I was texting with a long-distance friend, attempting to catch up on life in three hundred characters or less. You know how it is. Allison filled me in on how law school was going, then in the playful way so typical of her, added for good measure, "At forty, I am finally in my sexual prime!" My husband, Eric, was in the room, and laughing, I insisted on reading Allison's text message out loud to him. He arched an eyebrow and grinned in response, saying, "Did you tell her you are, too?" I think the second half of life was Teresa of Ávila's sexual prime as well. She just expressed it differently.

As we mature, we settle into an ownership of our bodily experiences and learn to grow comfortable in our skin, whether or not our bodies ever touch the intimate skin of another. As Teresa discovered at about age forty, sexuality can be deeply expressed in a multitude of ways, and in those ways we celebrate bearing the Divine image the way it deserves to be celebrated. We are less inhibited, more free. We are finally ready to appreciate pleasure and delight in the senses without the self-consciousness that plagued our youth.

And then, in the decades nearest the end of our life on earth, our sexuality morphs in form yet again, this time unleashing itself onto the world as a passionate energy to enact positive change. In her midfifties, Teresa led a small group of nuns within her convent who all shared a critique of the materialistic and frivolous spirit found within their walls. These women, joined by local laywomen, desired more serious prayer and community. By now it shouldn't surprise us that Teresa's passion for reform began to take root from human connection and deep, spiritual friendship;

all of Spain was changed by a handful of women sitting around a table, just talking about God.

The path from this humble beginning to the opening of the first reformed Carmelite convent took two years of lawsuits and threats from church authority; nevertheless, our saucy saint persisted. And then, after founding the first reformed Carmelite convent in 1562, Teresa of Ávila relentlessly traveled throughout Spain to trailblaze seventeen new convents that would be radical in devotion to their Beloved. Despite severe pushback, and even after her writing was turned over to the Inquisition, where it remained until her death in 1582, Teresa submitted herself to the process and let her theological insights speak for themselves. No longer tied to concern for herself or her own ego, the aging Teresa was freed to pour herself out for both the individuals she loved and the good of the Church. She knew body, soul, and spirit that she was acting in the will of God.

Following in Teresa's footsteps, may we, too, allow our sexual, sensory, embodied energy to propel us to make the world a better place. When it is our turn to enter the last season of life, may we unleash the desire for love and connection inside of us into the quest for the common good, honoring as we do so the future of our children—both natural and spiritual—and the legacy we wish to leave behind.

Questions for Prayer and Reflection

1. What was your experience with Christian purity culture, whether first- or secondhand? What effect did those messages have on the way you have understood your sexuality long-term?
2. How does it feel to consider that sexuality might encompass

something wider than strictly sexual pleasure or intercourse? What does the term *sensuality* evoke in you? How do you respond to the idea of sexuality and spirituality informing each other?

3. Consider friends or loved ones who express their sexuality differently than you do. What would it look like to honor those differences? What might doing so have to teach you about yourself?

MARGERY KEMPE

CHAPTER THREE

All the Best Prophets Were Mentally Ill

I had just turned eighteen when I started cutting my feelings right out of my skin. There was a boy, of course, and a star-crossed-lovers plotline, and probably one too many indie movies about troubled teens, but mostly there was just me and a safety pin and the irresistible imagining of how cathartic it would be to actually see my own pain. In the privacy of my bedroom and with the witness of a mirror, I carved his initials into my right hip, light enough not to draw much blood but hard enough to last a week.

This was the first time I cut, but it wasn't the last or the worst. I was already on antidepressant medication, which helped to manage the overwhelming feelings of despair and allowed me to have meaningful friendships and academic success, but which couldn't provide the instant relief that came from splicing my skin and watching in real time as my body reacted. Nor could it help me communicate my pain to others the way the red lines did in the rare instances that I chose to reveal them to someone I trusted. While I usually wore long sleeves to cover the marks, doing so was less because I wanted to hide them and more because hiding them seemed the thing to do.

Yet a part of me longed for the scratches to be noticed—for what they represented to be heard. Like many teenage girls, I struggled to know how to access and employ my own voice. I didn't think it could be trusted or that anyone really cared to hear it—at least not in its most honest iteration—and when you have no voice, other things must be substituted in its place. And in my freshman year of college, my most reliable substitution was to call into duty any sharp object I could find in my dorm room, scissors mostly, but also butter knives and once, while drunk and desperate, the corner of a glass picture frame.

I don't remember how my mom found out about my cutting habit, but I do remember she insisted that I see a counselor on campus, who proved to be a safe and helpful listener as I processed and made sense of the storm within. This counselor had me make a list of other, healthier coping mechanisms I could employ in moments of overwhelm, things like writing in my journal or calling my sister, which helped me turn a corner over time. Still, when I finally quit cutting, it was begrudgingly, like a smoker quits: knowing it was necessary but resenting that I actually had to do it.

But ending my practice of self-harm didn't magically make me mentally healthy again, and I knew it. I was a loose cannon, unpredictable and potentially hazardous. Quite frankly, I liked it that way. I once bought a T-shirt at Hot Topic (remember Hot Topic?) screen-printed with a picture of a bunny in a straitjacket. It said, CUTE BUT PSYCHO. THINGS EVEN OUT. I still remember the way my mom chewed her lip as I sashayed my way to the checkout.

By my sophomore year at my small Baptist college, I had earned a reputation for being a little unhinged, but it didn't bother me; if anything, I was even proud of it. I couldn't articulate it at the time, but somewhere inside I understood that being "mad" was about much more than my diagnosis of clinical depression—it was about social resistance. It was about refusing to be complicit in the bullshit of a world that grooms people into participating in their own dehumanization, disciplining them to be "well-adjusted," which means they must pretend that everything is fine when, really, nothing is fine. Pain, trauma, and injustice are so embedded into our idea of normalcy that we are culturally conditioned to numb them out. But I couldn't. I saw, and felt, everything.

During this time I had a boyfriend who told me I was crazy. When I pointed out that this made us a good match (ahem), he declared that he was "the cool kind of crazy" whereas I was—and here he made a mocking face—"just crazy." That was twenty years ago now, and his words still capture the gender bias in the public mental health conversation.

Despite the fact that mental illness is more common among women than men (26 percent of women in the United States experience mental illness, while 16 percent of men do), it is harder for women to obtain the medical care we need. A recent report from the national nonprofit Treatment Advocacy Center found that women's severe mental health symptoms are less likely to be taken seriously by clinicians and are more likely to be misdiagnosed than men's symptoms. The report also stated that there are larger barriers to treatment for women with severe mental illnesses than for men with the same disorders, right down to the number of beds available for women versus men in specialized centers.

But it's not just gender bias in the medical field that causes these added obstacles women face. The female form is subjected to intense social scrutiny; it is viewed, discussed, and capitalized on. A woman's place in our culture is a veritable breeding ground for body dysmorphia and eating disorders. What's more, even the natural female biological processes add a layer of vulnerability to the risk of destabilizing mental health concerns. Many of us experience dramatic mood shifts before menstruating every single month for our entire lives, and for a prolonged period during menopause. But these are at least culturally acknowledged phenomena, chemical realities that are accepted as happening *to* women, not caused *by* them. They might be the butt of misogynistic jokes, but they are also bonding agents for women. If there is shame attached to the mood swings of menstruation and menopause, it is at least an experience that women can bemoan together.

Mental health anomalies surrounding childbirth are another story.

Perinatal depression—that is, depression in the weeks before and after giving birth—affects a staggering number of women around the world, and yet as a society we are only just beginning to recognize and talk about it because we believe "good mothers" are not sad, overwhelmed, or ambivalent about life with their newborns. The Centers for Disease Control estimate that one in eight women suffer from postpartum depression, but as many as half go undiagnosed because they are too ashamed and afraid to speak of it. And postpartum psychosis—a more extreme mental health crisis after childbirth marked by hallucinations, delusions, and severe behavior changes—affects one or two out of every 1,000 birthing women. This sounds rare enough, until you hear that around 385,000 babies are born every day around the world. That means that at least 385 postpartum women experience terrifying mental breakdowns *every single day*.

In the year 1393, one of those women was Margery Kempe.

*   *   *

Margery Kempe was born Margery Burnham in 1373 in Norfolk, England. Her father's position as the mayor of the town of Lynn meant that the family, while not in the elite class, still enjoyed social favors and privileges (a reality that would save Margery's life more than once). Margery married John Kempe when she was about twenty years old and gave birth to fourteen children before she was forty. Yes, you read that right. She gestated and birthed fourteen children in twenty years.

By her own account, Margery's first pregnancy was brutal, marked by severe sickness from conception until delivery. While we can't know for sure, it is possible that what she suffered from is known today as hyperemesis gravidarum, an extreme and persistent vomiting that can lead to life-threatening dehydration. You might remember hyperemesis gravidarum entering public discourse in late 2012, when Princess Kate was hospitalized in the United Kingdom during her first pregnancy. But the Europe that Margery Kempe knew had no IVs at its disposal.

As if nine months of severe sickness wasn't trial enough, Margery suffered from a mental breakdown after delivering the baby, terrorized by visions of both Jesus and demons. She later described being out of her right mind for months, unable to perform daily tasks or care for her infant. Her symptoms are consistent with today's diagnosis of postpartum psychosis.

When she eventually recovered, Margery vowed to be a good wife and mother. She loved her family and had every intention of being a decent and respectable homemaking woman. But there was one tiny snag in the plan: Margery was feisty as hell.

Like so many passionate women who marry young, Margery struggled to balance self-discovery and self-development with the demands of running a household and raising children. She enjoyed fashion and beauty and took pride in her physical appearance, even admitting in her autobiography that she felt envious of her neighbors if they were dressed as well as she. (Note that she didn't say "better than" but "as well as." Reader, we bow to a petty queen.) Sure, in her vanity we see youth and immaturity. But we also see a young woman, full of life, who refused to waste away as an aging matron in a dark house.

Margery bridled this life energy and ran with it. Possessing an independent and entrepreneurial spirit, she single-handedly pioneered two business endeavors, a successful brewery and a rather less successful horse mill, all while continuing to birth babies at a staggering rate. Her life was full and, by all accounts, pleasant. Then something happened that would change everything.

One night as Margery lay in bed with her husband, John, she had her first mystical experience, hearing "a melodious sound so sweet and delectable that she thought she had been in paradise." The sound she heard was every bit as real as the sound of John's voice beside her. Margery jumped straight out of bed and shouted, "Alas that ever I sinned! It is full merry in heaven."

Continuing her account of the incident, she writes (in third person), "This melody was so sweet that it surpassed all the melody that might be heard in this world, without any comparison, and it caused this creature when she afterwards heard any mirth or melody to shed very plentiful and abundant tears of high devotion, with great sobbings and sighings for the bliss of heaven, not fearing the shames and contempt of this wretched world. And ever after her being drawn towards God in this way, she kept in mind the joy and the melody that there was in heaven, so much so that she could not very well restrain herself from speaking of it. For when she was in company with any people she would often say, "'It is full merry in heaven!'"

Though she had always been religiously devout, in this single moment Margery was forever ruined for anything less than the divine Presence. She would spend the rest of her life seeking and savoring that Presence, because the sound from heaven had rendered everything else unimportant.

I wish I could say I have experienced a similar mystical moment myself. The closest I've come was when once, in a time of earnest prayer, I suddenly smelled an extravagant floral scent. Here was my much-longed-for supernatural encounter, I was sure of it: I was smelling the aroma of heaven! Then I opened my eyes and saw a vase of roses two feet to my left. End scene.

But I do believe that these things happen, times when the veil between what we call heaven and earth thins and blurs. I love to hear stories about such moments. When I read Margery Kempe's account of what she heard, and especially her reaction to it ("It is full merry in heaven!"), I was reminded of the way my friend Laura speaks of the most transcendent experience of her own life. Laura is among the many of us who live with a proclivity toward melancholy and depression, but the most formative moment of her life was quite the opposite. It is what she calls the time she touched The Joy.

A few years ago Laura endured the trauma of having to say goodbye to her premature twin daughters, Maggie and Abby, mere days after their birth because they suffered from twin-to-twin transfusion syndrome and surgery had failed to save their lives. Maggie died first, safe and loved in Laura's arms. The next day Laura woke up knowing she would have to do it all over again: this time, hold Abby in her arms as her second daughter died. Hold a universe of grief and pain yet again. How can a woman survive such a thing?

But strangely, it wasn't grief and pain that met Laura when she held Abby skin to skin that day. It was hours of pure, blissful paradise. Laura described it this way on her blog:

I could not conjure a single sentiment of sadness. I could not remember why I had wept when we said goodbye to Maggie, when we knew this perfect joy was what awaited her. . . . This was heaven stretched out for hours. . . . We were right inside the heart of God. . . . And if I could share only a sliver of what it felt and breathed and loved like in that NICU room, you would never again fear any doubt of the divine or the existence of an afterlife. I am certain of this.

Margery Kempe called it "full merry." Laura calls it "The Joy." Mystics have called it other things for centuries, but one thing is for sure: it is a taste of ultimate reality, a taste of the eternal, a taste of that which exists but cannot yet be seen. And I do not think it is a coincidence that the ones who catch glimpses are often the ones who would get red-flagged during the requisite mental health assessment at the doctor's office.

After all, everyone knows the best prophets were mentally ill.

*   *   *

The character sketch of the outlandish prophet is a running joke among Bible nerds, of which I suppose I am one, having attended two Baptist colleges and a missions training school. But even before my formal education with Scripture, I spent many a preadolescent weekend traveling across the state of Texas for Bible Drill competitions in the hope of being the first of the lineup of ten-year-olds to put my finger on Luke 11:9 the moment the judge began reading, "Ask and it will be given to you . . ."

Yes, I am a Bible nerd, and somewhere in a dark corner of my parents' basement I have the watermarked nineties certificate to prove it. But back to my point. If you know your Bible, you know that the biblical prophets are whack. Just total nutjobs. The weirdest of the weird of society. Ezekiel had bizarre visions, physically ate a scroll, lay on one side for over a year, and cooked food over a fire of turds. Isaiah walked around Jerusalem naked for three years. Jeremiah wore a yoke over his shoulders and hid his dirty undies under a rock. I could keep going. These are not history's normies we're talking about here.

What fascinates me is not so much that such people have always existed but how nonchalantly our religious spaces accept their spiritual work as valid. No one really questions their prophetic legitimacy, even in the face of some eccentric and, at times, downright disturbing behavior or speech. We are satisfied with the stamp of approval that time and tradition have conferred, a stamp first bestowed in a social landscape which recognized that the work of the Spirit often defies what we find sensible. It's ironic that even while we continue to accept such historical prophets with ease, we would never take them seriously today. Their prophetic roles worked only because the people of Israel in their time understood that such roles were valid, even necessary.

In many cultures today, there is still space carved out in the public sphere for the prophets: the shamans and medicine people, the seers and dreamers, the poets and priestesses. Such individuals do tend to exist on the margins of the community, likely because of their eccentricities, sensitivities, and possible neurodivergence, but these communities nevertheless recognize that such persons play a vital role for the common good. Indigenous and nonindustrialized cultures tend to be quick to honor the voice of the prophet as crucial for their wholeness.

But in our Western culture it is a different story. Here we tend to organize our religious experiences around order, credibility, and boundaried belief—things that don't exactly welcome the prophetic imagination. While there is a certain wisdom to not entrusting serious spiritual matters to only a few select "holy" people, there is also a grievous loss in our rejection of the role of the prophet. And there is an abundance of prophets who feel rejected by their church.

Despite great gains in the public consciousness when it comes to understanding and integrating mental health, we still have far to go as a society, and, tragically, religious institutions are often lagging the furthest behind. In many churches and other places of worship, stigmatization of mental illness is alive and well, shaming folks into silence and disqualifying many from leadership positions. Perhaps the most dangerous thing about this attitude is that it is often framed as a sin issue: anxiety as a failure of trust, depression as a failure of gratitude, personality disorders as character flaws or, in more charismatic spaces, demonic strongholds.

Given the wealth of scientific information at our disposal, this kind of ignorance is *bananas*. And yet, here we are. An acquaintance of mine recently recounted that during her child's freshman orientation at a Jesuit university, a priest told the auditorium full of teenagers that anxiety was a lack of faith. These are the same teenagers who had just weathered a global pandemic in their most formative social years. Teenagers who were leaving home for the very first time. Teenagers who needed comfort and encouragement, not shame and condemnation. If anyone had sinned in this scenario, it was that priest.

Many of us have our own stories to tell. I have friends who have been advised by pastors not to enter therapy because therapists will try to undermine their faith. We have all heard reports of pastors, church elders, and boards of directors discouraging the use of medication for mental health disorders, wanting their leaders and parishioners to "get to the root" of the problem in prayer instead. These were never things I heard in my own moderate Protestant upbringing, but the bias was still present in the omission of things like counseling and antidepressant medication from discussion and, in some cases, consideration.

As for me, while I never cut myself again after quitting, bouts of depression have continued to cycle through my life in nearly predictable rhythms: when my husband and I lived in Southeast Asia as missionaries, when I became a mother for the first time through adoption, and then again later after delivering two unplanned babies in a row. By now I have accepted that medication will be an indefinite part of my spiritual life. Praise God for the sacrament of Zoloft.

Perhaps the reason appropriate discussion about mental health is so taboo in many Christian circles is that we have excluded from leadership those who can personally speak to it. When people with mental or emotional fragility are dismissed as delusional and untrustworthy, the prophetic imagination of the group withers and dies. For without a finger to the pulse of suffering, of longing, of need, we are subject to devoting everything we have to answering questions the world isn't even asking. We need the prophets—the artists, the highly sensitive people, the deep feelers, the discerners. We need them to point to where the world hurts. We need them to point to where *we* hurt. We need them to tell us the truth.

* * *

From the night that she heard the heavenly music, Margery Kemp made union with God the business of her life: it consumed her thoughts, informed her choices, and steered her desires. She became enamored with theology and spiritual conversation and spent as much time as she could at the local church asking questions of the priests and confessors. Her commitment to an informal religious education, coupled with her everyday mysticism, gradually won her favor in the eyes of those in authority, and before long she found herself with something of a public ministry. But more than anything, she desired to go on spiritual pilgrimage. You don't have to be a mother of fourteen to appreciate what a pipe dream that would have been for a married woman in the fifteenth century.

And yet, against all odds, this particular woman was stubborn enough to make it happen.

In 1413, at age forty, Margery took matters into her own hands. She left her children—including an infant—with her own mother, nannies, and her husband and embarked on a pilgrimage that would keep her away for five years.

A few months into her journey, Margery and her travel companions made it to the Holy Land. When their tour following Jesus' footsteps climaxed at Mount Calvary, Margery burst into uncontrollable tears from thinking about his pain and suffering. This was the first time she had experienced such crying while in contemplation, but it would be far from the last. For the next ten years of her life, Margery would be ravaged by daily bouts of weeping.

Often this weeping would occur during prayer or when she was talking or thinking about the Passion of Christ. But other times, it was seeing the suffering of Christ in humanity or in the natural world that would bring the ungovernable tears to her eyes. She writes, "Sometimes, when she saw the crucifix, or if she saw a man had a wound, or a beast, whichever it were, or if a man beat a child before her or hit a horse or other beast with a whip, if she saw or heard it, she thought she saw our Lord being beaten or wounded, just as she saw it in the man or in the beast." But it wasn't just the suffering of humanity that made her weep; it was the beauty, too. Margery describes being transported into such states while attending weddings or witnessing a woman undergo ritual purification after childbirth. Margery saw the Holy Family (Mary, Joseph, and Jesus) in our shared human experience, and the sacredness of it all rendered her unable to stand.

Unsurprisingly, her fragility made other people uncomfortable. Margery describes being the target of contempt, accused of every slanderous explanation under the sun: people said she had a demon, that she was cursed, that she was drunk, that she sought attention, and that she was ill. People said they wished she would sink to the bottom of the sea. (Sounds like a medieval Twitter troll to me.) Though some select spiritually minded individuals believed she was touched by God, the tender voices were rarer than the cruel ones.

Because she was a woman in public ministry, preaching in the streets, Margery's precarious mental and emotional state gave everyone from commoners to church authorities an invitation to ridicule, mock, dismiss, or threaten her. She was written off by many as an attention-seeking, hysterical woman. Some priests and bishops accused her of purposefully leading other women astray and publicly cautioned them not to follow her. As too often happens to people with mental health difficulties today, there were many who refused to take her seriously as a spiritual teacher because she was different. But that didn't stop Margery.

The bouts of weeping might have caused social and relational pain for Margery, but the weeping itself was not burdensome to her. On the contrary, she found herself craving it. She had no power to bring on these episodes, but when they did come she welcomed them as friends. When they were absent for a day or more, she actually longed for them. They made her feel God's presence. They made her feel alive. They made her *feel*. She understood that the weeping was a gift.

Once, Margery was brought before the Archbishop of York and a panel of male clerics to be investigated for heresy. As she prayed to God for help against her enemies, she fell into a weeping episode right then and there. "Why do you weep so, woman?" the archbishop gruffly demanded to know. Margery Kempe looked right into the eyes of the most powerful man she had ever encountered—one who would determine whether she would live or die—and answered, "Sir, you shall wish some day that you had wept as sorely as I."

It is not that Margery took masochistic delight in her misery. On the contrary, the weeping spells were not misery to her at all. While there were plenty of people who urged her to hide away in shame, Margery refused to let her condition debilitate or disqualify her. On the contrary, she was a prominent spiritual teacher and pilgrim as well as a devoted wife and mother. And rather than stay shut away for fear of embarrassment, she chose to accept herself, frailty and all. Day after day, Margery lifted her chin and did the brave thing of allowing others to see what she might have kept hidden away in her inner life; she allowed her life to become a window into the divine Presence that had touched her—and she did so in the public eye.

And the public eye of the Middle Ages desperately needed Margery's courage—just as the public eye of today needs the courage of all prophets, poets, artists, and dreamers. For these are the voices moving us forward. These are the voices that re-fuse to let us stay stuck, the ones that pull us out of complacency

and offer us a baptized imagination for all that the world could
be, for all that *people* could be, for all the love we have too long
withheld that we could offer.

Questions for Prayer and Reflection

1. As you revisit your own mental health history, what feelings do
   you notice arising? Shame and embarrassment, or sensitivity
   and curiosity? What factors might influence those feelings?
2. How have you been complicit in the silencing of honest discussion about mental health?
3. Have you ever observed or participated in the dismissal of
   spiritual leaders with precarious mental health? How might
   their conditions have been approached more holistically?
4. What experiences or observations do you have of sexism in
   mental health discussions and management?

CHAPTER FOUR

How to Become a Virgin Again

> Therefore a man leaves his father and his
> mother and clings to his wife, and they become
> one flesh. *(Gen. 2:24, NKJV)*

Attend any religious wedding ceremony and you're likely to hear this reading from the book of Genesis. For that matter, many nonreligious weddings use it, often adapted into something more generic about "two becoming one." In either case, it is in our cultural lexicon to describe the romantic ideal of finding that special someone and creating an entirely new identity with them, leaving the old life and loyalties behind.

But if taken at face value, the words of Scripture—"they shall become one flesh"—really seem to be about sex. Because, uh . . . biology. And yet we have interpreted this passage to mean two individual humans who are so committed to each other that each is willing to forfeit an autonomous identity in order to create a brand-new, enmeshed version of themselves, like some kind of toxic conjoined twin.

If you ask me, it's time for a renewed examination of this cultural adage. Because if "two become one," what happens to the pieces left over? If "two become one," won't there always be a half that takes up more space and a half that curls itself up to make room?

I have been married for close to two decades, and for most of that time I never questioned the whole "two become one" thing. Like most Americans, I accepted that the ultimate ideal of marriage was unity. Cohesion. Oneness. For that, they say, is what makes a strong marriage. That, we are promised, is what will safeguard the relationship from pain and see it through the long haul.

So I tried; God knows I tried. I have a black belt in codependency, and I did my damndest to fuse myself to my spouse. I tried to preserve unity at the expense of honesty. I tried to share everything: schedules, interests, beliefs, opinions. Eric never asked for this, but like so many women before me in this world, I understood that it was my lot in life. If "two are to become one" then something has to give, and women know that that something is us. So we give and give and give, until we either lose ourselves permanently or break. And long live the women who survive the break, for theirs is the kingdom of God.

* * *

Not long after her mystical experience of hearing the "full merry" of heaven, Margery Kempe told her husband that she wanted to take a vow of celibacy in order to fully devote herself to God. In her own words, Margery wrote, "After this time she never had any desire to have sexual intercourse with her husband, for paying the debt of matrimony was so abominable to her that she would rather, she thought, have eaten and drunk the ooze and muck in the gutter than consent to intercourse, except out of obedience."

At this point in our cultural consciousness, I sure hope we can all agree that the word *obedience* has no place in discourse about marital sex. It is painful to see a woman so sure of her own feelings be forced into sex against her will in the name of wifely duty. And yet, let's be honest, this perspective is still alive today. But keep reading, because it gets worse.

"And so she said to her husband, 'I may not deny you my body, but all the love and affection of my heart is withdrawn from all earthly creatures and set on God alone.' But he would have his will with her, and she obeyed with much weeping and sorrowing because she could not live in chastity."

Right here, in the first memoir ever published by a woman in human history, we have irrefutable evidence of marital rape. Sexual trauma was one of the first stories women had to tell.

It does not matter that Margery and John might have mutually enjoyed an active sex life in the past. Consensual sex is not an unlimited contract; it is a case-by-case decision. Margery drew a boundary and her physical, emotional, and spiritual self was violated who knows how many times. In her story, we see the cross women have carried since time immemorial: the underlying belief that our bodies belong to men. In her story, many of us see ourselves.

Remember also that Margery was getting pregnant and giving birth in a near-constant cycle during this time. Not only was she the victim of repeated rape but also she carried the physical reminder of her sexual enslavement at almost all times. There is no reason to doubt that she loved every one of her children—and likely even loved John—but pregnancy and childbirth can be debilitating under the best of circumstances. And these were not those.

Margery asked her husband not to rape her for three or four years before he relented. She tells us, "Her husband said it was good to [abstain], but he might not yet—he would do so when God willed. And so he used her as he had done before, he would not desist."

This is spiritual abuse on top of sexual abuse. Spiritual abuse invokes supposed authority from God in order to manipulate the victim into performing something that meets the needs of the abuser. Cult leaders infamously do this with their devotees. Televangelists do it with their donors. But it happens on more mundane scales, too; and in the Kempes' case, it was in the marriage bed. So long as John, the supposed spiritual head of the household, claimed that God had not spoken to him about celibacy, he was free to continue raping his wife. Her voice, will, desire, and ability to discern God's voice for herself were considered irrelevant.

But let's be clear; John Kempe was not an evil man. In other places in the book we see him lend great support to his wife and her uncommon spiritual endeavors, believing in her calling with sincerity and loyalty. This was a pretty radical thing for a husband to do in the Kempes' day. John was not a devil; he was an entitled man in a patriarchal society. No one in the Middle Ages would have questioned that he had the right to demand sex from his wife. The problem wasn't one bad apple, the problem was that the entire orchard grew—and continues to grow—around the using and discarding of women's bodies.

Finally, after years of forcing himself on Margery, the fear of God struck John Kempe and he agreed to her pleas for a shared vow of chastity. In a time when a woman had essentially two life paths, the one to the convent or the one to the marriage bed, the idea of a celibate wife and mother was as strange as it is now. And since the vow was made under the authority of the Church, it was public knowledge. People called Margery a disgrace and made her life a living hell by their taunts and jokes. But it didn't matter to Margery Kempe. All she cared about was that—at last—she was free.

* * *

My own awakening to the call to self-belonging was a gradual one, a slow rollout of consciousness and conviction that a younger me had once exchanged for social safety and acceptance. A few years into the process—after publishing a book titled *Rewilding Motherhood,* and long after the time I thought I should have this all figured out—I entered a frightening season of facing my ache for freedom head-on.

For several months I felt like I was crawling out of my own skin, day in and day out. I wanted to run naked on all fours through the woods behind our property. I wanted to leave home and travel the world alone. I wanted to buy my own house on our street and forge some new arrangement of the modern family, putting a dramatic stake of independence in the ground.

None of it made sense. Our marriage was better than ever; Eric and I were best friends and (wink) extremely compatible lovers. Our five kids were out of the baby stage, and parenting was slowly getting easier. I had a meaningful job that gave me great satisfaction. We had just bought a dream house beside forest and prairie. Where were these urges coming from? I felt a little guilty for not being satisfied with so many blessings; but much more, I felt enlivened by the possibilities that my body and heart were beginning to name. It was both embarrassing and exciting all at once. I had just finished reading *The Book of Margery Kempe* and felt a kinship with this eccentric patron saint of self-belonging. I understood her and felt she understood me. If she could leave her family and go on pilgrimage around the world, anything was possible!

And yet, I didn't want to hurt the ones I loved. No shade to Margery, but in my case it didn't feel necessary, ethical, or healthy to just take a leave of absence from my family for a few years. Was there a way to integrate the contradictory parts of myself? Was there a way to honor my most primal desires without imploding my family?

Luckily for me, my therapist is trained in a method called Internal Family Systems (IFS), a model of psychotherapy centered on the principle that the mind is naturally multiple. An IFS approach is a practice of giving attention and voice to each part of ourselves to experience integrated healing. Considering that I felt like multiple people residing in one body, this method came into my life right on time.

When I was invited to imagine the part of myself that was restless, wild, and thirsting for freedom, the form of a wolf came to mind. I spent many a therapy session talking to and about this wolf-me. I wrote her letters in my journal and read the letters "she" wrote back to me. She told me about all the ways I've caged her and I told her she can't have free rein over my life. She told me she's afraid of being killed, and I told her I'm afraid she'll kill everything I hold dear. I listened to her; she began to trust that I would. Gradually, we moved toward integration.

The wolf and I talked a lot about her feelings concerning marriage, or, more accurately, her feral reaction to the threat of belonging to anyone. We all have our reasons for the shadows that haunt us, and I came to understand—and have compassion on—wolf-me's belief that loving a man meant losing myself. I even came to appreciate wolf-me and the hell she raised, because without her feisty grit I would have continued to suffocate myself needlessly.

As I processed all this with my spiritual director one day, she recommended a book called *Passionate Marriage*. I admit, I was skeptical at first; marriage books have never carried much resonance for me and tend to leave me with a bad taste in my mouth. But I trusted my spiritual director, and after reading just the prologue, I was sold. This wasn't a book about "communication" or the importance of "dating your spouse," none of those obvious pieces of marriage advice we've all heard a thousand times. This was a book about how to maintain your own person-hood in a committed partnership—and how that self-validation actually makes the marriage hotter. Now that's a book to pique a couple's interest!

Passionate Marriage was what first led me to question the nar-rative of "two become one." Healthy marriages, author David Schnarch maintains, are those in which two are able to remain two, not become one. Emotional fusion will rot a relationship from the inside out; differentiation keeps us healthy and protects us from resentment. Schnarch likens it to sailing on a lifelong journey: if two individuals are tasked with piloting one boat, the experience will inevitably be marked by competition for control, bickering about how things should be done, and a desperate need for personal space. But if each party has their own sailboat and they are committed to traveling side by side, these problems are minor or nonexistent. The journey can be enjoyed, not just survived.

I started evaluating my personal history, on my own and in therapy, to understand why and when I had decided that enmesh-ment and codependency were my life's fate. Once I understood the why, I could begin to ask, *So now what?*

For months, I did the work. I felt the grief. I developed the resolve. I had the conversations. I set the boundaries. I accepted critique and owned my mistakes. I had compassion for my inner child. I stopped projecting old wounds onto assumptions about my spouse. I exited the single sailboat we'd been trying to conavi-gate and hopped aboard the one waiting with my name on it, promising to keep traveling with the man I love. At nearly forty years old I started to really believe that I could love another, be a partner for another, and still belong to myself. At nearly forty years old, I became a virgin again.

*   *   *

Renowned psychiatrist Carl Jung based much of his work on the theory that certain archetypes are consistent across all human cultures and individuals, and that they serve as patterns, offering us insight into how to move forward in our lives.

For example, the most popular archetype in our storytelling canon is that of the Hero, whose trajectory is marked by courage, risk, self-sacrifice, and facing death (think Frodo, Luke Skywalker, and Harry Potter). But there are many other archetypes that merit equal attention, one of the most important among them being the Virgin.

In Jungian thought, the Virgin represents the art of Becoming and Being; hers is the quest of knowing, trusting, and expressing her truest self without compromise. Kim Hudson, author of *The Virgin's Promise,* says, "The Virgin must answer the question: Who do I know myself to be and what do I want to do in the world, separate from what everyone else wants of me?" Unlike the Hero, who must set off into a foreign land to find his resolution, "the Virgin confronts her central question in her childhood environment with its teachings and expectations because these are the forces that compete in her mind as she seeks to define herself as an individual. Her journey is towards psychological independence."

While the Hero and the Virgin are obviously masculine and feminine archetypes, they are not relegated to strictly male and female experiences; people of all genders are likely to live out various archetypes at different points in their stories. But in my years of writing and speaking in female-dominated spaces, I have found that women overwhelmingly identify with the Virgin archetype. We can assume this is because we are more broadly

conditioned to remain perpetually dependent, whether materi-
ally or psychologically; not to mention the fact that there are
real social and relational consequences for women who refuse
to be people-pleasers. The task of stepping into self-belonging
is riskier for females.

There is also the matter of the stigma associated with a woman
pursuing her own joy and liberation. Because of our high regard
for courage and sacrifice, the cultural reward for the Hero—male
or female—is great. But there is a collective side-eye for the pursuit
of self-fulfillment when it means disappointing others or trans-
gressing established authority, even and perhaps especially the
authority of nonverbal cultural agreements. For instance, when I
write about the self-giving required of me in motherhood, I find
I am commended and praised; yet when I write about the tension
of pursuing my own passions while raising children, I am often
cautioned against letting such things interfere with mothering.

But the truth is, we all need both the Hero and the Virgin
to emerge in our lives. We need both self-fulfillment and self-
sacrifice—and we need wisdom to know when to exercise which.
This is why storytelling matters. Hudson writes, "The need for
an understanding of the Virgin becomes profound when it is
recognized that archetypal stories are roadmaps for life. We need
to be more than brave, self-sacrificing Heroes. We also need to
be Virgins who bring our inner talents and self-fulfilling joys to
life. And we need stories that show us how to do that."

*   *   *

Not long after finally taking her vow of celibacy, Margery Kempe
made plans to embark on a grueling pilgrimage across multiple
countries. This was a rare venture for any woman of her day, rarer
still for a married woman without her husband, and astronomically

rare for a mother. The dangers of sexual assault, robbery, and death were acute and very real. Survival often depended on the keeping of a low profile and the loyalty of one's fellow pilgrims.

So naturally, Margery Kempe insisted on dressing head to toe in white like a virgin and traveled with a group who mostly despised her.

The all-white ensemble was an instruction from God, Margery believed, and it only contributed to the prevailing public sentiment that she was off her rocker. She was no virgin, the haters cried. How dare she wear white?

This is my personal favorite among the many controversial choices Margery made in her lifetime. The vow of celibacy meant so much more than not having sex with her spouse anymore; it was a stake in the ground of self-belonging and self-fulfillment. Would Margery have described it that way? No. For her, the apex she sought was to give herself over to God and God alone. But despite what they may seem, these things are not contradictions. For when we are our most true selves, we are most fixed in divine reality. When we trust our sincere inner compasses above external authority, we are attuned to the push and pull of Spirit. Our most authentic self-belonging is actually God-belonging.

So it's endlessly fascinating that what Margery Kempe identified as being given fully to God tracks so well with the Jungian archetype of Virgin. (I would say she also took a Hero's journey, but that's a story for another day.) It is a powerful confirmation of the connection between body and spirit, as well as between self and God. And it's interesting to note that dress plays a specific part in the archetypal story line.

In her extensive Jungian-informed research on the Virgin, Kim Hudson identified "Dresses the Part" as an established stage on the Virgin's journey. And if you think about it even for a minute, you'll see evidence of this fact in stories everywhere, from *Cinderella* to *The Princess Diaries* to *Pretty Woman*. Hudson says, "Before the Virgin can consciously relate to the invisible energy of her authentic self, that energy has to be transformed into something tangible. Once her unconscious dream becomes visible, she will never be the same again."

As fulfilling as dressing the part felt to Margery, it made her a magnet for public scorn—and not just from common townsfolk. The white dress disturbed several men in power, for a woman who did not abide by social rules was a woman they could not control. And if other women got wind that this was a possibility, who knew where it would end?

The Mayor of Leicester, well-known to be a wicked man, once called Margery in for questioning. "I want to know why you go about in white clothes," he said, "for I believe you have come here to lure away our wives from us, and lead them off with you."

(Insecure much, sir?)

Margery was not having it. "Sir," she said, "you shall not know from my mouth why I go about in white clothes; you are not worthy to know it." And after a burn like this our crafty queen continued on to come up with her own solution by offering to explain it to her trusted priestly confessors, who could then report her reasons back to the mayor.

When she later appeared before the Archbishop of York, a much more severe threat than the mayor had been, he asked her the same question. "Why do you go about in white clothes? Are you a virgin?"

"No, sir," she answered. "I am no virgin; I am a married woman."

The archbishop then ordered her to be chained up for heresy, to which she replied with trembling hands, "I am no heretic, nor shall you prove me one." After this the powerful man brought in a slew of clerics, monks, and doctors to question and examine her. Finally, they had to admit that she was not in heresy, but they forbade her from teaching or speaking publicly of God; in fact, they demanded she swear she would not do it. "No, sir, I will not swear to it," she answered. "I think that the Gospel gives me leave to speak of God."

Such confidence should have had her neck, but Margery's biblical knowledge backed up every claim she made. She was brought before authorities and threatened with death so many times that the reader of her memoir loses count, yet her actions and words could not be undermined. No fault was ever found.

*   *   *

After years of being stripped of bodily autonomy and self-determination in every possible way, Margery Kempe finally found a path to return to herself. In reclaiming her physicality as an outward sign of an inward state, she found a means to embody a disembodied concept—and then adorned her flesh in a color that would signify to the world that she would be acting in accordance with her deepest conscience from that moment on.

This doesn't mean she abandoned her marriage or motherhood. The path of the Virgin can look many different ways; but being an internal movement, it often means things more or less appear the same from the outside. After her lengthy pilgrimage, Margery returned home prepared to hold the tension between being faithful to family and staying true to her calling as a spiritual leader and teacher. We aren't privy to the details of the family arrangement, but Margery most likely resumed her place as mother to her children. The vow of celibacy between her and John Kempe continued for the rest of their lives, to the gossip of the town, who would shame the wife for the fact, but Margery was devoted to her husband nonetheless. When John fell ill in old age, Margery nursed him until his death.

What Margery Kempe touched, even without having specific language to articulate it, is the Virgin archetype within each of us, which beckons us to belong fully and completely to ourselves. To not suffer others who want to tell us how and where and when to experience God, but to commit to our own unique relationship with the divine through accessing the deepest, most true parts of ourselves.

Margery stands as history's Stella Maris for every woman who feels she's lost and drowning in the sea of who she "should" be, how she "should" think, and the ways she "should" behave. For us, Margery lifts a lantern, letting the beams of her light pierce the darkness of the storm, urging us not to give up on the quest, promising that what is inside us is enough for us to reach the shore.

Questions for Prayer and Reflection

1. What are examples of the Virgin archetype in some of your favorite books, movies, or fairy tales?
2. At what times in your own life has the Virgin archetype come out?
3. How do you approach the balance of self-fulfillment (Virgin) versus self-giving (Hero)? Which comes more naturally to you? Which is calling for your attention at this time?
4. How have you experienced being disempowered or victimized in your body? How can you pursue greater healing through physical, embodied practices?

HILDEGARD OF BINGEN

CHAPTER FIVE

Spirituality Demands Environmental Justice

My family's home altar is, frankly, pretty weird. There's a Guatemalan crucifix hanging on the wall and a bottle of holy water atop the little table, but traditional Catholic imagery ends there. The rest is made up of our love offerings to and from a God of creation: snakeskins and snail shells, and dried flowers, and butterfly wings, and hawk feathers, and a raccoon skull. Treasures the seven of us have collected in the woods behind our house, reminders of the questions nature poses: *Who made this? How does it hold together? What comes after death? Can the Source of life be trusted?*

Oscar, four years old, runs through the open back door with a dried wasps' nest in hand, eyes sparkling. *Look,* he breathes, *something to make us think about God!* In his lispy enthusiasm, I recall the words of Pierre Teilhard de Chardin: "I worship a God who can be touched, and I do indeed touch him."

A wasps' nest. A goldfinch feather. A smooth stone. Such are the sacramentals of a prairie Mass. When the whole world is an altar, every twig is a talisman.

But here in the West, our theology recognizes no such altar. Oh sure, people of faith are good at giving lip service to the importance of environmental stewardship, but only until it breaches our worship of convenience. Once justice for the earth requires some of our ease, some of our comfort, we draw the line. A 2022 study released by the Pew Research Center found that most adults in the United States consider the earth to be sacred and the care of creation to be a God-given duty. But the study also found that Americans who identify as highly religious (i.e., those who report praying daily, attending religious services regularly, and consider religion to be crucial in their lives) are far less likely than other U.S. adults to express concern about climate change.[*]

Divisive political rhetoric has convinced many conservatives that climate change is a hoax, and many highly religious individuals are also politically conservative. But the disconnect can't be pinned on politics alone; the study found that many of those surveyed who were not concerned about climate change held their ground under a vague belief that "God is in control of the climate."[†]

Meanwhile, we shoot prayers to heaven like missiles and hope they land in the ear of "the Big Guy upstairs." For too many of us in the modern world, concepts of God, heaven, and eternity are far removed from the ins and outs of our daily experience. We are experts at compartmentalization and have a long, rather dreary, history of separating the spiritual and the material, the spirit and the flesh, the sacred and the secular.

If God is *up there* and we are *down here,* then we are forever relegated to live oblivious to the pulsing of Spirit through the earth and her creatures. What a tragedy it is that we believe prayer means closing our eyes and hoping to be transferred to a far-off place, when right here and now we have the presence of

[*] "New poll shows religious Americans worry less about climate change," *Earthbeat,* A Project of *National Catholic Reporter,* November 17, 2022.
[†] Ibid.

God at our fingertips. What a shame to shoot requests off into the stratosphere when the trees overhead offer divine revelation and this, too, is prayer. When this, too, can fill us with faith.

Where, oh, where are the prophets who would soften our craned necks and tilt our chins downward from the sky to the earth?

*   *   *

Hildegard of Bingen was given as a tithe to God.

Born in 1098 in the Rhine Valley of Germany, Hildegard was the tenth child of a noble family. Her parents, Hildebert and Mechtild, knew well the ancient Rhineland custom of tithing their tenth child back to God, so when a teenager from a local highborn family entered religious life, Hildegard's parents offered their eight-year-old daughter as a companion for Jutta of Sponheim. Jutta proved a faithful mentor for Hildegard, and our future saint took her monastic vows at just fourteen years old.

Far from a normal story, certainly; but then, Hildegard had never been a normal child. As a very young girl she had begun to experience visions that overcame her body, the details of which so unnerved her parents that she learned it was best to keep silent about her encounters. In fact, Hildegard spent half her life resisting her rare gifts of mysticism and leadership because, due to her gender and lack of education, she couldn't conceive that her calling could be legitimate.

As is true of many of our most compelling female mystics, Hildegard didn't really step into her power until midlife. After more than half a lifetime of trying to quell her encounters with what she called the "Living Light," at forty-three years old she heard a voice commanding her to write down what she was experiencing, not out of self-indulgence but for the benefit of others. There was no precedent for female theologians at this time, and the thought of stepping into the role made Hildegard physically sick. But she did it. She did it with stomach churning and knees quaking, but she did it all the same.

And you have to hand it to the gal; once she was in, she was *all in*. Hildegard of Bingen wrote theological books, preached to both laity and clergy, counseled popes, pulled her female religious order out from under the authority of a supervising male order, and traveled far and wide preaching on the urgency of church reform. She had no patience for hypocrisy and zero qualms about calling anyone out on it.

But her religious accomplishments only begin to scratch the surface of her contributions to society: she also wrote plays, composed music, created her own language, made medicinal discoveries, and wrote the first scientific discussion on sexuality and gynecology from a female perspective. You know, just little things like that.

Hildegard is one of the most accomplished women in history, yet she wasn't declared a saint and doctor of the Catholic Church for her contributions to Christian theology until 2012—nearly a millennium after her death in 1179 at age eighty-one. Why the long wait? Well, if you've made it this far in the book, you won't be surprised to hear that Hildegard made a lot of folks uncomfortable. In fact, she still does.

There has been no shortage of voices throughout history that have called—and continue to call—Hildegard of Bingen a witch, pagan, or dissident. After all, she concocted "magical" herbal remedies, healed ailing bodies with crystals, and openly defied the authority of bishops and other male clergy. To the skeptics, it doesn't matter that Hildegard was an orthodox Christian and even rather conservative in some of her beliefs and opinions. She was and is a *dangerous* woman in a certain sense of the word, for the combination of female brilliance, self-trust, and confident voice is a veritable hat trick with the power to defeat spiritual gatekeeping.

It's noteworthy that the misogynistic energy that seeks to dominate and discredit women like Hildegard is the same as that which dominates and disregards the earth. In her book *Gaia & God: An Ecofeminist Theology of Earth Healing,* the late Catholic feminist theologian Rosemary Radford Ruether points out that the historical subjugation of women to men is not dissimilar from the subjugation of earth to humankind. And Ruether says the Western tradition has sacralized these relationships of domination, calling this hierarchy the immovable will of God.

"The idea of the male monotheistic God, and the relation of this God to the cosmos as its Creator, have reinforced symbolically the relations of domination of men over women, masters over slaves, and humans over animals and over the earth," writes Ruether. "Domination of women has provided a key link, both socially and symbolically, to the domination of earth, hence the tendency in patriarchal cultures to link women with earth, matter, and nature, while identifying males with sky, intellect, and transcendent spirit."

Oh snap. When you look at it this way, it's no surprise that humanity has abused and discarded the earth—the same thing happens to women every day. When we buy into the line that God's ways are hierarchical rather than interconnected, those on the lower rungs of the ladder will always suffer at the hands of those at the top, who see dominion as not just their right but their calling. It's Margery Kempe all over again. If it's not a woman being raped, it's the earth.

*   *   *

The impacts of climate change are accelerating so quickly that any statistics I cite are sure to be old news by the time this book is published. But a 2022 report from the UN's Intergovernmental Panel on Climate Change (IPCC)* urged world governments to take appropriate legislative actions in the next twenty years to hold global warming to 1.5 degrees Celsius, the magic number for minimizing loss and damage to both human systems and ecosystems.

But even if we manage to hit and maintain that magic number by 2042, between 3 and 14 percent of the earth's species face a "very high" risk of extinction. We're talking best-case scenario here! With the loss of so much biodiversity, ecosystems will suffer and weaken. And imbalanced ecosystems have less chance of adapting to a changing climate. It's a pretty bleak picture—but the alternative is much worse. As one expert put it in an interview with the *National Catholic Reporter,* the IPCC report "makes painfully clear that the cry of the Earth is at its highest pitch yet."[†]

And it's not just animals and ecosystems that are suffering; people are, too. The regions most vulnerable to the impact of climate change—those that already suffer under poverty, unstable governance, and limited resources—always seem to be the regions least responsible for it. For example, the IPCC report found that while the continent of Africa produces a mere 3 percent of global greenhouse emissions, it represents more than half of all human deaths from climate-related illnesses.[‡] This is a social justice issue if ever there was one.

If right about now you're feeling like throwing this book

---

* *Climate Change 2022: Impacts, Adaptation and Vulnerability. Working Group II Contribution to the IPCC Sixth Assessment Report*

[†] Ibid.

[‡] Ibid.

across the room and crawling into bed for three days, I don't blame you. I get it. And maybe that's okay to do every once in a while, but at some point we have to get out of bed and start making choices again: choices about how to transmit outrage into output, despair into dedication.

This is precisely why we need leaders like Hildegard of Bingen in the environmental justice movement. For without spiritual rootedness, we will either burn out in bitterness or give up and do nothing. We simply can't fight for the earth without letting the earth fill us first.

Hildegard had a sacramental way of seeing the world. To her, the material and the spiritual were two sides of the same coin. Matter, flesh, earth: anything her senses could process contained and communicated God and was regarded with deepest reverence. In fact, arguably her best-known spiritual principle is the idea of the earth as a sacred mirror reflecting our internal reality. Central to her understanding of God's spiritual work in nature is what she called *Viriditas*.

Viriditas, or the "greening power" of the Divine, is the force of the Spirit that is actively moving all things—including you and me, just as much as the earth itself—toward wholeness. *Viriditas* is a becoming. The greening power of God means that nothing is final; everything is in motion, everything is in process. It means that the very forces of creation, rebirth, and fertility that keep the earth in motion are also living and active inside of us, because the greening power of God dwells within each of us. We are constantly being reborn, constantly being reimagined, and the earth plays that cycle out before our eyes as a way of bearing witness. Just as the seasons come and go, so do the highs and lows of our lives: the cold and the warmth, the light and the dark, the death and the rebirth. It all holds, because we are all held.

In keeping with this sacramental lens, scholars have noted that Hildegard's writings put more weight on the incarnation (God becoming human) than on the crucifixion and resurrection of Jesus—quite a departure from the prevalent Christian teachings of her day, which emphasized sin and atonement. Hildegard didn't seem terribly concerned about whether she or anyone was going to hell; she was too busy enjoying heaven on earth, where "divine love . . . abounds in every grain of being, from atom's gleam to starry sky."

It's not that Hildegard was flipping the bird to Christian orthodoxy. That wasn't her style. It's just that she believed that if we could see the dignity and sacredness of our cosmic interconnection, we would be less likely to be ensnared by sin; for love and relationship will always produce better outcomes than fear and shame.

But it wasn't a matter of rainbows and unicorns and rose-colored glasses for Hildegard. She believed in a Christian cosmology because she believed in science. And though there are naysayers on both sides of the aisle, I have to believe that if we dive deep enough into either science or spirituality, we will eventually run into the immovable reality that life and love are one massive web of interconnection.

Naturalist and ecophilosopher Lyanda Lynn Haupt says this belief is the thread running through all kinds of mysticism, expressed by the most revered mystics of various religious and spiritual traditions around the world. In her book *Rooted,* Haupt writes, "Mystical insight and ecological science are mutually reinforcing—both refer to an underlying unity that dissolves the notion of an absolutely separate individual."

And yet most of our Western culture—particularly our religion—teaches us otherwise.

* * *

As for far too many women, sexual assault is a part of my story. It took fifteen years for me to be able to say that, and this is the first time I've ever written those words in a book. And while at first glance a chapter on environmental justice may not seem like a very intuitive place to start, I would beg to differ. The bodies of women will always be mysteriously intertwined with the body of Mother Earth, and reconnecting with the earth is a consistently proven way to soothe the effects of trauma on our minds and bodies.

Speaking of bodies, one of the most grievous wounds of sexual assault is that it robs us of a healthy embodiment. The way it's been explained to me is that in order to protect us, our brains distance themselves from reminders of trauma, and when trauma is experienced in your body, that means your earnest, protective little brain decides that the best way to move forward is to disconnect from the very body you're living in. And when we are disconnected from our bodies, we will inevitably also be disconnected from our intuition. We ignore the red flags waving in our guts and mistrust our own evaluation of things. Instead, we look for someone else—often someone in a position of authority—to interpret the world for us.

That's how, at twenty years old, I found myself in the deep end of the evangelical charismatic pool, committed to a local church community (accused by many of being a cult) that vehemently espoused beliefs and practices I would have never embraced before the assault. I now understand that, unconsciously, I was looking for safety; and nothing promises safety quite like a rigid religious subculture.

I attended church-related functions multiple times a week:

Sunday morning services, weekly small groups, midweek college student services, volunteer opportunities, you name it, I was
there. Butt in the seat. *For years.* And that's not even counting the
national conferences, prayer gatherings, concerts, and the like,
because you know my spiritual-bypassing ass was at all of those,
too. And in all of that time, not once did I hear anything about
climate change—or even anything vaguely resembling serious
concern for the environment. If I rake through the cracks and
crevices of my brain, I want to say there is a memory or two in
there about the virtue of picking up litter, but that's about it. I
sincerely hope my experience was the exception rather than the
rule in evangelical churches; but frankly, I'm doubtful.

For reasons having nothing to do with global warming, I
left evangelicalism in my late twenties, and my husband and I
made our unlikely way into the Catholic Church. Now, Catholicism has a list of problems a mile long (where is my award for
understatement of the century?), but one thing it has done well
is emphasize the moral duty to care for creation. Shortly after
I became Catholic, Pope Francis released the papal encyclical
Laudato Si': On Care for Our Common Home, which presupposed
the validity of climate science and called all people of faith to
take immediate action.

Although my radical Catholic anarchist friends bemoaned
what they saw as a tepid message from the pope on a critical
issue, my own bar had been set pretty low back in college. I was
just impressed that anything was being said at all. And while
Catholic spirituality can vary widely among regions, parishes, and
individuals, I have been pleased to hear climate justice preached
in homilies and to see action groups formed in both urban and
rural areas across the United States in the past decade. And just
a few years ago, the Vatican unveiled the *Laudato Si'* Action

Platform, a centralized way to offer the global church tools and resources for the journey toward total sustainability.

When I reflect on the stark differences between my experience in two faith traditions under the same Christian umbrella, I can't help but notice the way theology informs the posture of each toward climate change. Theology that puts more emphasis on the individual falls prey to the illusion of separateness from the environment. For if we're just looking out for our own personal relationship with God, biding our time with morality until we die or are raptured off the earth, then it's pretty hard to take seriously our impact on or responsibility to our planet.

On the other hand, theology that centers the whole of humanity is more readily postured to see and act upon the human connection to earth as well. Catholicism is far from the only faith tradition to emphasize the common good, but it has been the one to take root in my own life, so it makes for a convenient example. The point is not that we should all be Catholic, but that we all have access to a more attuned, holistic, inclusive theology no matter our formal religious tradition, or lack thereof. As our belief system matures, it should expand beyond "me" into the realm of "we."

The Franciscan Father Richard Rohr teaches that there are two halves of life: in the first, he says, we are tasked with creating a healthy ego structure built on identity, security, and a sense of importance; in the second, we are freed from those very same things. What results is a faith that evolves from something egocentric into something more intangible that encompasses everything. What we call our faith goes from being a belief system to defend to being an experience to savor; and when that happens, we find the divine worth savoring everywhere.

But we cannot will this shift into happening; we can be open and malleable only when it does. Perhaps it is enough to start by walking out the door, sliding your toes through the dirt, and moving worms onto the grass so they don't fry on the sidewalk. Because after all, your backyard is a sanctuary, your dirty toes are Good News, and who knows, that worm on the ground might be as Christ to you. As we remove ourselves from the center of our worldviews and step back into the broader interconnected tapestry where we belong, we will gain a truer understanding of the vastness of this love we have so long sought to know.

It surprised me to learn that the Christendom of Hildegard's day was better at this perspective than we are today. (Please tell me I'm not the only one snobby enough to assume modernity always equals superiority.) But theologian Elizabeth Dreyer writes that in the twelfth century, a renaissance of spiritual and intellectual curiosity produced a widespread reverence for the earth. "Old ways of viewing the relationship between the supernatural and the natural worlds gave way to a new awareness of the integrity of nature," she writes. "The world remained connected to God through creation and God's ongoing presence, but divine activity was seen more in terms of the workings of nature itself, rather than primarily through supernatural beings or movements. . . . The world was viewed as connected in all its parts."

And so with her sacramental view of the world, Hildegard of Bingen was a true woman of her time. Speaking from the perspective of God in *Book of Divine Works,* she wrote: "I gleam in the waters, and I burn in the sun, the moon and the stars. With every breeze, as with the invisible life that contains everything, I awaken everything to life. . . . I remain hidden in every kind of reality as a fiery power. Everything burns because of me in the way our breath constantly moves us, like the wind-tossed flame in a fire."

In such words we hear whispers of what is popularly associated with Francis of Assisi, who would come around a hundred years after our trailblazing nun. Both saints spoke of the earth and her creatures as living things cohabitating with us humans within the great divine life. When Francis spoke to "Brother Sun and Sister Moon" in his now-famous canticle, there was no hierarchy to be found. He was not above creation; he did not speak of dominion or even benevolent caregiving. Mystics like Francis and Hildegard understood that there is no pecking order in the bosom of God. All life is God's life.

So where does that leave us today? There is no single right way to take action on climate change. Some will run for public office, some will organize nonviolent protests, some will create sustainable technology, some will run organic farms, some will sit on boards of directors. But most of us won't do such big things. Most of us will cast our vote, call our representatives, struggle with our gardens, and try to remember to turn out the lights when we leave a room.

All of those things matter. (Yes, even calling your representative and enduring that horribly awkward two minutes of lodging your complaint with their poor plebeian staffer while hoping they won't press for details because you didn't memorize every point of the bill you are calling to oppose. Yes, even this matters.) But there are things that matter more.

Actually spending time in the nature you are trying to save matters more. Intimately knowing your own native trees, plants, and flowers matters more. Having a conversation with an oak tree; saying "pardon me" to the garter snake you nearly stepped on; kneeling down to pray beside a river; these things matter more. Bringing your broken heart to a marsh; asking her to heal you; promising to heal her back. These things matter more.

Why? Because these things bring about true conversion. Because we can't really give a damn about the earth unless we recognize why we need it; how it's a part of us—the best part of us, really. The part of us that is wild, primal, instinctual, trusting. The part of us that cries when we read a Mary Oliver poem without fully understanding why. The part of us that is homesick for who and what we were meant to be. Without knowing our home, we will never know ourselves.

"We know that there is more than what has been given and named by the overculture," writes Lyanda Haupt. "More than green gardens and nature calendars, and recycling, and a summer hike in the mountains, and an occasional camping trip. More, even, than an hourlong 'forest bath,' however lovely that sounds. We know there is a wilder earth, and upon it—within it—a wilder, more authentic human self. *We know the need of each for the other is absolute.*"

This is the prayer of Hildegard of Bingen for us in this climate change generation: that we would know our need for a wilder earth is the need for a wilder self is the need for a wilder God. For it is all one spirit, one love, one strand of golden thread woven through time and space. May we find a way to forever keep weaving the tapestry, on and on and on.

Questions for Prayer and Reflection

1. It is said that Hildegard of Bingen had a sacramental view of the world. What does that mean to you? Do you personally identify with that description of faith? Why or why not?
2. Was environmental justice a part of your faith formation? If not, why do you think it was omitted? If it was, did it take root in you?

3. How do you perceive the connection between women's bodies and spiritualities and the earth? Do you agree with Rosemary Radford Ruether that sacralizing the domination of women has given us permission to also sacralize the domination of the earth?

CHAPTER SIX

The World Is Burning: Why Make Art?

I can remember the exact moment when I first identified as a writer. Despite having written in one form or another since childhood, and despite the fact that at the time I was writing regularly and sometimes even making a tiny bit of money doing it, I had never had the courage to claim the title for myself. But on this particular day, as a newcomer to the town we now call home, an acquaintance asked me what I did when I wasn't busy mothering. When I explained that I wrote a blog, contributed to spirituality websites, and was having my first print article published in a magazine soon, this woman rightly assessed, "Oh, so you're a writer."

It seems so obvious, no? But I stammered, insecurity tying my tongue. Finally I sheepishly smiled as I confirmed that yes, I was a writer.

I can only imagine how shocked this friend would be to find out now that this was actually a formative conversation for me; but there is no rhyme or reason to what will stick in our brains and continue to make its mark years later. (Meanwhile, I can't remember what it was I walked upstairs to retrieve this morning once I made it to the top of the landing.) For me, this seemingly insignificant conversation made an impact: a virtual stranger had called me a writer, and I had confirmed it. Claiming the title felt a little like when I was a child and would play dress-up with my mom's jewelry: awkward and clunky, but pleasant.

Why is it so hard for women to claim our creative identities? I don't mean the professional artists; I mean those of us who don't have an MFA or a photography business or a byline in *The New Yorker*. I mean the women who squeeze creating into the cracks and crevices of our days, not because we have the credentials or the platform or even necessarily the talent, but because we are creative creatures, compelled to spin something out of nothing. Compelled to make tangible the things we have to say.

One of my best friends, Cameron, is a gifted writer but, like me, suffers from a certain degree of imposter syndrome. More than once she has moaned to me, "If only I had the confidence of a mediocre white man!" It makes me laugh because as an editor for a national newspaper who sifts through countless submissions each week, I can attest to the reality. Men—yes, especially white men—do not seem to question whether their work is good, whether it is legitimate, or whether the world needs it.

There are exceptions, naturally; I'm married to one of them. (And I wouldn't say that if it weren't true.) But by and large, the stereotype exists for a reason. Centuries of human society have assured men that their public contributions are necessary and welcome, while the opposite has been true for women and has only relatively recently begun to change. So we are still finding our footing, still feeling risqué when we dare to stretch out and take up space. If you're really digging deep and doing it right, artmaking by its very nature is scary and vulnerable for anyone— exponentially more so for women.

In *Big Magic,* her fantastic book on living the creative life, author Elizabeth Gilbert notes that many of us avoid making art—or downplay it when we do—because our artmaking feels arrogant. Who are we, we reason, to devote time, energy, and resources to something other people can do better? Who are we to ask the world to give it their time and attention? It is all too easy to convince ourselves that our artistic impulses are egotistical. And once we've gotten that far, it takes almost nothing to decide to abandon them.

Yet Gilbert asks us to flip the script on where lies the real navel-gazing. She observes that "often what keeps you from creative living *is* your self-absorption," and by that she means "your self-doubt, your self-disgust, your self-judgment, your crushing sense of self-protection."

Reader, I ask you: does anyone do self-doubt, self-disgust, self-judgment, or self-protection like a good woman does self-doubt, self-disgust, self-judgment, or self-protection? I would wager that the more of a "good woman" you are, the less likely you are to be making the kind of art that you really want to make.

Oh, I don't mean *good* in the sense that you don't drink or do drugs or have never stepped foot in a nightclub. I mean *good* in the sense that you don't let anyone down; you defer to authority; you meet expectations; you do what you're told to, think as you're told to, and avoid what you're told to. This, quite frankly, is how women are conditioned in much of the world, so if you see your reflection in these sentences, then you are in excellent company. For many of us, being seen as arrogant or selfish is the most heinous of crimes and one that we have orchestrated our entire lives to avoid.

I have a big ol' juicy bone to pick with the assumption that a woman's highest virtue is selflessness (why do we communally exalt the loss of self?), but I also find balance in the truth that no one likes an egomaniac. But hear ye, hear ye: good girls, gather round.

What if Liz Gilbert is right? What if repressing your creativity is actually the arrogant thing? What if the truly generous thing is to make your art and offer it to the world—whether that's on your windowsill, on your friend's wall, or on a billboard in Times Square?

It begins by defining yourself, by declaring your intent. Just as I experienced that day years ago when I simply agreed, "Yes, I am a writer," naming and claiming your identity out loud carries a powerful energy. Maybe for you it's saying, "I am a dancer," or "I am an actor," or "I am a painter," or "I am a chef." Whatever it is, whatever creative title you long to claim, try it out: say it out loud to yourself. Write it down and look at it. Speak it to someone around you. Introduce yourself that way to the next person you meet. Try it on for size and see how it fits.

"This statement of intent is just as much an announcement to yourself as it is an announcement to the universe or anybody else," Gilbert writes. "Hearing this announcement, your soul will mobilize accordingly. It will mobilize ecstatically, in fact, because this is what your soul was born for."

* * *

Hildegard of Bingen never seemed to question what her soul was born for. In dramatic contrast to the norms of her time, Hildegard was a woman who *did* have the confidence of a mediocre white man. When it came to creative pursuits, Hildegard waited for permission from no one but herself. She didn't demur; she didn't downplay; she didn't repress. This woman unleashed her wild, wise imagination with everything she had in her—and the world is still talking about it.

Hildegard is famous for many things: science, music, drama, painting, natural healing, poetry. An impressive array of talents, but all of them art—and, for Hildegard, all of them sacred practices. For she was equal parts artist and theologian: she created because she couldn't know God and not create. She made art because without it all her spiritual language came back void, all theory and no substance. Curiosity begets curiosity; love begets love.

When you are swept up in the great eternal story of the love that exists among all things because of one Great and Ultimate Lover, the result is generativity. The energy of love is never static: it is always moving, always birthing, always creating. And when we, like Hildegard, put a toe in that river, we, too, will be swept away from our egos, swept away from the arrogance of self-doubt, into the current of generativity.

Hildegard may have been a naturally confident woman. She may have been a woman who was raised to believe that her voice and perspective mattered. She may have been entitled, being from a noble family; maybe she was even spoiled. It's true that some of her trailblazing acts of creativity were likely results of both nature and nurture. But I have to believe that much of her art also grew from her claiming an identity as Beloved: beloved by God, beloved by the earth, beloved by its plants and creatures. She found her identity as part of the whole, and when your life becomes more than about you, withholding your gifts just seems silly and selfish. Why would Hildegard refuse to give good things to a world that gave such good things to her?

For those of us who struggle with imposter syndrome, or who feel we haven't yet earned the right to self-identify as artists, or who stumble over the thought that there are so many more important things to do before making art, Hildegard of Bingen is the patron saint we need to be praying to. Being Catholic, I do believe that we can pray to saints and ancestors and earnestly expect them to come to our aid. They're the communion of saints, the great cloud of witnesses, whatever you choose to call them. From the official vantage point of the Catholic Church, Hildegard of Bingen is the patron saint of ecology, music, and writers. But she is not limited to those fields, so feel free to call on her for all your needle felting and underwater basket weaving needs as well.

Because honestly, what *is* art, anyway? Weren't Hildegard's homeopathic remedies just as much art as her musical compositions? They required the same creativity, the same imagination, the same experimentation. Who gets to decide where the line is drawn? If you've never thought of yourself as an artistic or creative person, perhaps that's less a reflection of your internal reality and more a reflection of our too-small definitions.

A few months into the coronavirus pandemic, when we were all popping our anxiety meds and despairing of ever returning to normal again, a tweet began circulating on my social media feeds. I don't know who @jishyouwish is, but we have them to thank for this gem:

"As you binge watch your thirteenth entire series or read a book or sleep to music, remember. Remember that in your darkest days when everything stopped, you turned to artists."

You see, art is a much wider and sneakier thing than the forms to which we reduce it. We limit our conception of artists to those whose work hangs in museums or galleries, or maybe a symphony hall or poetry book. We take for granted the art forms ingrained in our cultural rhythms: Netflix shows, the latest Marvel movie, Top 40 radio. These, too, are art, even if some are bad art. They are the art forms woven into the fabric of our everyday lives. Most of us do not own expensive paintings or attend orchestra concerts, but we all seek out art to quiet our fears and console our hearts.

It's no wonder that during the early stages of the pandemic lockdown so much of the country became obsessed with watching

Tiger King and baking sourdough bread. When the world grows heavy, we turn to storytelling and the act of creating; we turn to depictions of humanity and our persistent determination to live and not die.

I like to think these motivations were on Hildegard's radar, too. I like to think that she made art because connection matters; because she shared our need to know that at the end of our darkest day there are others asking our questions, sharing our fears, and clinging to our hopes. If there is anything worth giving time to, if there is anything worth being stubborn about, if there is anything worth looking for God in, isn't it that?

*   *   *

When you are new to the boldness of giving yourself permission to make art, one of the most important demands to attend to is finding your voice. This can be tricky if you are a woman, and doubly tricky if you are a woman who was raised in a home or culture that expected you to read from a certain script.

Claiming your own voice—your own perspective, your own experience, your own intuition, your own prophetic call to the world—is essential for artmaking. Really finding your voice, and learning how to trust and use it, is one of the most radical things a woman can do. It is also one of the most creative things a woman can do, whether or not you ever consciously plan on creating a damn thing in your life. Because I promise you this: if you use your authentic, God-given voice, *something* will be birthed. Your voice is too generative, too fruitful, for it to be otherwise.

Think about it. Why was it voice that was taken from Ariel by Ursula in *The Little Mermaid*? (As a fairy tale junkie I am pained to use the Disney names instead of the Hans Christian Andersen identifiers, but I am not oblivious to my minority status here, so we're going with Ariel.) Ariel had determined to take the biggest risk of her life, make herself vulnerable in every possible way for the sake of love (and, more important in the actual story, eternal life; but again, I'm trying to stick to Disney here). Why would Ursula demand her voice, of all things? Why not her gorgeous hair, or her sweet disposition, or her great rack?

Because the sea witch knew that voice equals power. It equals agency. It equals fortitude. Able to take only one thing in the little mermaid's possession, Ursula was no fool about what to do. She chose the most consequential.

I remember the year in my life when I came to see I had lost my voice. I was in my midthirties, and, once the fog lifted, I realized I had willingly let myself become voiceless by parroting the voices of those around me. It was a survival mechanism, and it had done its job admirably. But I was no longer willing to settle for survival. I realized I was sick of being an Ariel, fighting tooth and nail to make my own way without the one tool that I needed for my journey.

Recently I was talking with my therapist about this—both that specific season of my life and the fact that it's still a work in progress for me—and she disclosed that the same thing is true for most of the women she sees. Not only that, but the awakening tends to happen at the same time of life, between a woman's midthirties and her midforties. With fifteen years of counseling practice under her belt, she could testify to something I had intuited from observing myself and my peer group: women, we have a massive Ariel crisis on our hands. And we've got to wrestle our voice boxes back.

David Bayles and Ted Orland, authors of the book *Art & Fear,* use the term *vox humana,* and I'm going to employ it here because, frankly, I think it sounds badass. If you're familiar with Latin at all, it's not hard to figure out that *vox humana* means "the human voice." Bayles and Orland have this to say about it: "To make art is to sing with the human voice. To do this you must first learn that the only voice you need is the voice you already have."

Sit with that in a spirit of honesty for a moment. Are you trying to channel someone else's voice when you make your art? Do you remain unconvinced that your voice is interesting enough, important enough, strong enough, palatable enough? Have you yet learned that the only voice you need is the voice you already have?

I would add a caveat, though, for the sake of brutal honesty: sometimes our voices can be hella boring. Sometimes our voices don't push boundaries, don't elicit change, don't inspire thought. Sometimes our voices are safe. Sometimes they're a snooze.

In my own creative journey, I have found that the times my own voice has bored me—the times I have gone searching for another's voice to use instead—are the times I have become complacent, played it safe, and been too timid to push the boundaries of my own thought and imagination.

Sometimes the culprit is the imagined audience. What would they think if my art veered toward the avant-garde? Or acknowledged the existence of sex, violence, injustice, or any other social faux pas? What if it was controversial? What if it (gasp) didn't sell? Too often, we imagine the discomfort of those possibilities and choose instead to stay within the lines, deliver what feels safe, and settle for a lame voice and subpar art.

Our creativity deserves so much more. Our audience (whether one person or one million people) deserves so much more. As artists, as creative vessels, we deserve so much more. One of the greatest gifts of artmaking is that it helps us find our voice. But that is not a onetime event. We must refind our voice every day.

Every day. Every day. Because there are too many forces in the world that would have us zip our lips instead.

One way we can find our most compelling creative voice is by asking questions. Bayles and Orland write, "The people with the interesting answers are those who ask the interesting questions." No one embodies this truth better than Hildegard of Bingen. That woman was clearly asking interesting questions—geez, she was asking interesting questions about *everything*! And you know what? Both her art and her theology proved it, which is likely why her work makes so many people uncomfortable.

Hildegard's interesting questions about the interconnection between the earth and the human body birthed interesting answers about nature's healing properties. Her interesting questions about the sounds of heaven birthed interesting answers manifested in her own musical compositions. Her interesting questions about the Holy Spirit birthed interesting answers that assumed the Spirit is a She.

The point is not to be interesting for the sake of being interesting. I think it's safe to say Hildegard would be mortified if that were my takeaway for us. No, the whole point of interesting questions begetting interesting answers is that it all leads us to our voice. But we will never find that voice if we don't allow ourselves to ask the questions.

My surrogate godmother (no, she is not aware of this) Mirabai Starr says this:

"Have we longed to paint or sculpt the beauty that swirls behind our closed eyes but have been waiting for the last child to graduate from college before we allow ourselves to create art? Do we only make a joyful noise unto the Lord while singing along with the radio in the car, hiding our unique sound from the rest of humanity? Speak out, Hildegard says. And when you recognize that inner voice as the voice of God and say what it has taught you, the sickness in your heart will melt away. . . . To speak your truth, Hildegard teaches us, is to praise God."

*   *   *

With art, there are always two creative experiences. One, that of the artist; and two, that of the one encountering the art. They cannot and should not interpret a piece to the exact same end. The whole magic of art is that it shape-shifts to speak different things to different hearts.

The other side of that coin is that for the artist, there are always two creative fears: the fear about yourself, and the fear about how your art will be received by those who encounter it. The authors of *Art & Fear* sum it up this way: "Fears about yourself prevent you from doing your *best* work, while fears about your reception by others prevent you from doing your *own* work."

The era of social media explosion is a tough time to be an artist. Back in the day, artists were subjected to critique from only a small percentage of the general public, those who ran in the same circles or whose lives intersected with the work somehow. These days, being an artist inevitably means needing a social media presence—which then means your art is subjected to the critique of everyone and their random uncles.

The upside to this development is that small artists are gaining increased exposure, finding new opportunities, and often building viable careers out of thin air. But I fear the cost is the loss of courage. It is not an easy thing to live under the scrutiny of the masses, knowing that at any given moment someone can leave a single comment that will send you spiraling all day. It's easier to play it safe, to avoid risks, to stick with what sells. And this, my friends, is the elephant graveyard where art goes to die.

Art and rebellion have always gone hand in hand. Sure, there's the cliché of the rebel artist who is strung out on drugs and sleeping around, but that's only surface-level stuff. The real rebellion of art is the courage it takes to push back against the status quo, to make us think just a little bit differently, to challenge our perception of ourselves and our world. In the words of author and therapist Rollo May, artists are "the bearers of the human being's age-old capacity to be insurgent."

In *The Courage to Create,* May observes that artists "immerse themselves in chaos in order to put it into form, just as God created form out of chaos in Genesis. Forever unsatisfied with the mundane, the apathetic, the conventional, they always push on to newer worlds." This, he says, is creative courage—and it is demanded of us by artmaking if we are to remain true to the calling. It is exhausting and vulnerable and scary and disheartening. But it is necessary.

So get in touch with your inner insurgent, your inner rebel. Because we need you to tell us it can be better than this. We need you to tell us what the world could be.

*   *   *

At the end of her life, Hildegard of Bingen did her best to tell us what the world could be. As abbess of her monastery, the elderly nun had given permission for the body of a deceased young nobleman to be buried in the monastery cemetery. The circumstances are unclear, and we can't know her reasons for saying yes, but we can infer that Hildegard surely knew this would be a disruptive and controversial move.

Sure enough, she was ordered by the Archbishop of Mainz to dig up and remove the corpse from the cemetery. (I know, yuck.) The archbishop was angry that the nobleman had been buried on the monastery grounds because he had not been in an official "state of grace" in the eyes of the Church. Hildegard refused to disinter the man. By her own account, the nobleman had made himself right with God before he died and so deserved as much as anyone to be buried in a holy place.

The best part? Not only did Hildegard not comply but our sneaky minx actually went so far as to obscure the burial site so that no one else could do the job either. The image of this shrunken, eighty-year-old woman casually strolling through the monastery cemetery in her habit, messing with headstones and kicking brush around, delights me to no end. Just out there doing the Lord's work.

But, of course, open defiance of an order from the archbishop was not going to go unanswered. As punishment, he placed an interdict on Hildegard's entire community, forbidding the women from celebrating the liturgy or Divine Office (i.e., chant, song, ritual, and even the Eucharist).

Could the archbishop have come up with a more pointed punishment to wound a woman like Hildegard than to forbid the sacred song and visual beauty that had long ago become the scaffolding of her life? She who had written down the heavenly music that played in her soul so that, all these generations later, we are still singing her songs and playing her melodies? What cruelty!

By now, you won't be surprised to hear that Hildegard didn't take this lying down. She immediately replied with her own message to the bishops, warning them of the perils that awaited those who silence God's praise. But there was no change. For a month, two months, three, four—for nearly a year, Hildegard wrote letter after letter, stating her case. Finally, the interdict was lifted and song returned to the monastery. The abbess died not long after, surrounded by the sacred music that had marked her life. And in every woman who has ever fought for her art—fought for her voice—Hildegard lives on.

Questions for Prayer and Reflection

1. Think about the ways you exercise your creativity. How do you make art? In your life, has artist been an easy identity to claim or have you felt hesitant about it?

2. If "fears about yourself prevent you from doing your *best* work, while fears about your reception by others prevent you from doing your *own* work," as Bayles and Orland say, which fear holds you back the most?

3. What does your unique perspective, your voice, bring to your world through your art? Are you generous with your creativity?

JULIAN OF NORWICH

CHAPTER SEVEN

The Divine Feminine Isn't
Just Permissible, It's Necessary

In the dominant religious traditions of the West, God's pronouns
are "he/him." And since these religions (Christianity being the
most notable) have deeply formed our culture, even people who
aren't religious can be surprisingly adamant about the impos-
sibility of God being a "she." After all, we worship a Father and
Son, right? No mention of a Mother and Sister.

Even our tongue-and-cheek cartoons of God depict an old
white man with a long beard. Apparently this is our spiritual
inheritance, left to the mercy of the graphics team on *The Late
Show with Stephen Colbert*. But there's reason to hope that the
Spirit is doing a new thing. In fact, if you've been paying attention, there's a good chance you've noticed a change in the air:
interest in the divine feminine is skyrocketing. So much so, I'd
call it a cultural moment.

Out of curiosity, before sitting down to write this chapter, I
scrolled through the podcast app on my phone to see how many
podcasts would come up if I searched for the words *divine feminine*.
Among predictable titles like "Rise of the Divine Feminine," and
"The Mystical Feminine," I can report that there are podcasts
currently available for "The Divine Feminine CEO" and, my
personal favorite, "The Jesus Witch." If you are looking for a

podcast on the divine feminine, you have over one hundred to choose from.

A quick scan of Amazon offers even more confirmation: over four thousand book titles came up in my search for the words *divine feminine* on the website. Sure, some of them look a little bit kooky. But many more are seriously legit: Joseph Campbell's *Goddesses,* for instance, and Christena Cleveland's *God Is a Black Woman.*

But my guess is that you've noticed the rising interest in your own circles as well. Maybe you've seen quotes on your social media feeds that refer to God with feminine pronouns. Maybe your book club read and discussed Sue Monk Kidd's *The Book of Longings.* Maybe you've come across some beautiful art that depicts the feminine side of the divine. Maybe none of that has happened but you've nonetheless noticed a spark—a yearning— inside your soul that flickers and brightens and asks *what if?* when you let yourself imagine.

It really comes as no surprise that our collective unconscious is longing for a feminine God at this particular point in history. Gender inequality continues to plague our society. In the workforce, the gender wage gap is a real problem, as is the lack of appropriate maternity leave and affordable childcare. The #MeToo movement spotlighted the epidemic of sexual assault and harassment against women, filling our newsfeeds and conversations with the demand for justice, but it faded from headlines before lasting changes were made. When schools closed during the coronavirus pandemic, 1.1 million women were forced to leave the workforce to stay home with their children—a disproportionate number of the total jobs lost—raising questions about the disposability of women's labor and the injustice of patriarchal family arrangements. Since the dawn of social media, we are all more cognizant of gender injustices around the world: at the time of my writing this, girls in Afghanistan are prohibited by the Taliban from receiving an education higher than the sixth grade. Those realities take root in our worldview, even from afar.

It's a lot, am I right?

As all of this is swirling around us, many women have rightfully expected to find solace in our religious and spiritual spaces—only to find that there, too, the glaring injustices are inescapable. Men lead, preach, and teach while in many places women are formally prohibited from doing so. We stand and repeat words and sing songs about a God who is a "he," who is a "father," who is a "king." Our children go to youth groups where the girls are taught how to dress modestly and not cause the boys to lust. In the backs of our minds, we wonder if a man at the front of the room will be the next to make newspaper headlines for an affair or assault.

We go to our places of worship looking for the comfort we have always found there, but now all we feel is unsafe: spiritually, emotionally, and perhaps even physically. And when we start to pull on the loose thread, the whole cloak unravels, until we find ourselves limp and holding a tangled mass of knots, wondering where it all went so wrong.

In *The Dance of the Dissident Daughter,* Sue Monk Kidd describes having such an epiphany in the middle of a church service, fighting off tears as the congregation around her rose to sing "Faith of Our Fathers." She had already begun pulling on the loose thread, and the fabric could no longer hold together. "Until that moment I hadn't fully understood," she writes. "I was in a religion that celebrated fatherhood and sonship. I was in an institution created by men and for men. By the time I got home

I felt disbelief that I'd not seen all this before—that the church, my church, was not just a part of the male-dominant system I was waking up to, but a prime legitimizer of it."

If the maleness of God was established long ago and must be singularly upheld at all costs, we have to ask the question: *Who benefits from this?* If the divine, eternal, uncreated One has been packaged in exclusively male form, who benefits? Well, males of course. Because over the course of time, history, empire, and institution, the ones who "reflect" God to us are the ones with the power.

But what if it hadn't been so? Do we even have the imagination for an alternative? What if, long ago, someone had tried to tell us that God is more expansive than that? What if someone had warned us about being too narrow-minded and invited us to explore a whole other facet of the divine, an entirely new way to relate to the One we crave to know? What if someone long ago—someone trustworthy, someone with spiritual authority— told us that God is not only Father, God is also Mother?

*   *   *

Julian of Norwich is a woman hidden by history. We know she was an anchoress in the city of Norwich, holed up in a two-room cell that was literally built around her in the church. Anchorites, who were common in the Middle Ages, had their food (and Eucharist) delivered through a hole in the room and their chamber pots emptied the same way. Townspeople came to a window facing the street, bringing their spiritual matters to the holy woman, who spent her days in prayer.

Not much is known about Julian of Norwich's personal life, and she wanted it that way. We don't know the exact dates of her birth (somewhere near the end of 1342) or her death. We don't even know her real name. St. Julian's church in Norwich, England, is where she lived, and so its name was the only identity she took on. Even Margery Kempe referred to her as Dame Julian in her autobiography after seeking out the famed anchoress for spiritual counsel.

But anonymity did not prevent historical impact. Julian of Norwich experienced a series of sixteen fully embodied visions of Jesus in May 1373, which she referred to as "The Showings." Over the course of years, she compiled her notes on what she had seen and heard into a book entitled *Revelation of Love,* which she hid under her bed.

After her death a nameless protégée kept the pages safe, but Julian's work was lost to the folds of time for five hundred years. Finally, at the turn of the twentieth century, the book was discovered and realized to be the first book written by a woman in the English language—it came to be widely considered one of the greatest mystical works of all time. In it she covers a wide variety of topics, but none so unique as her perspective on Jesus as Mother.

My own introduction to Dame Julian was a winding road. I had vaguely heard of her, being a Catholic, but didn't know anything beyond her famous promise that "all manner of thing shall be well." But in 2018 the stage was set. We were still reeling from the fact that our country had elected an openly misogynistic man accused of sexual assault and marital affairs who bragged about grabbing women by our you-know-whats, and it turned out there was no rest for the weary. That August the Pennsylvania Supreme Court released a gruesomely detailed grand jury report of sexual abuse by Catholic priests that found over three hundred Pennsylvania priests guilty of having sexually abused more than one thousand children over the course of seventy years. Not since

The Boston Globe had exposed the depth of cover-up of the same abuse in Massachusetts had so much pain been unearthed for Catholics overnight. I was shaken.

That fall, President Trump had nominated Judge Brett Kavanaugh for the Supreme Court, and Christine Blasey Ford had come forward with allegations about sexual assault that she testified to having experienced at the hands of Kavanaugh decades before. The story permeated the news; everyone had an opinion about whether Blasey Ford was telling the truth, whether Kavanaugh was lying, and whether it had been too long ago to even matter.

While all this was happening outside, my own little corner of the world was being shaken, too, as the priest and bishop who oversaw the prominent women's ministry I wrote for decided I was too liberal and had to go. The book I had written with such love and devotion was pulled from the printer and trashed. My main source of part-time income—not to mention readership— was gone. Oh, and I also found out I was pregnant.

As fate would have it, this was all happening during a year when I had committed to a group going through the Ignatian Spiritual Exercises together for nine months. This model of prayer, written in the 1520s by Saint Ignatius of Loyola, encourages using your spiritual imagination to contemplate the life of Jesus by putting yourself in the scene and experiencing what happens in the story "firsthand." It is a way to pray that, with enough curiosity and self-honesty, can reveal things you may have buried within yourself. So our group would pray through the same Scripture passages during the week and meet every Tuesday night to share, without judgment, what had come up within each of us during our reading.

For the first few months, it was great. But the more my outer and inner worlds began to combust under the toxins of patriarchy, the more impatient and angry I became with the Scripture readings. I'll never forget showing up to one gathering where the discussion was on the Last Supper, the meal that Jesus shared with his disciples on the night before his death. I listened respectfully to everyone's flowery thoughts before deciding I had no more shits to give.

"I *can't* imagine myself in this story," I seethed. "Because there is no one like me in this story. Because according to this Bible, women were not present at the Last Supper or in the inner circle of bros. Trying to imagine myself in this story is incredibly painful."

A nervous silence filled the room. Everyone knew I was right. There was nothing more to say.

I went home that night knowing that something had to change. The old ways of approaching the Bible—of approaching the Christian tradition—were no longer working for me, and I couldn't keep pretending otherwise. I didn't want to leave Christianity, but for the first time I was allowing myself to acknowledge and feel the ache of exclusion that women try so hard to ignore. But it wasn't just my own ache I was thinking about. After four sons, I was pregnant with a daughter. And I'd be damned if I would raise her to believe she was a second-class citizen in her own faith. I was now on a quest on behalf of both of us.

I ordered a few books that had caught my eye as the feelings of prior months had snowballed, starting with *Untie the Strong Woman* by Clarissa Pinkola Estés (a book I actually slept with like a security blanket more than once) and *The Dance of the Dissident Daughter*. I am not by nature a theologian, but I familiarized myself with enough Elizabeth Johnson and Rosemary Radford Ruether to see a theological case for a feminine expression of the Christian God. Perhaps most important to my inner journey was the retreat I somewhat randomly found myself on, with a group of women I didn't know, that was grounded in the divine feminine. There I witnessed for the first time the joy and vitality that blossom when women gather together with the freedom and safety to swim in the waters of a God in whom we can see ourselves. The power of that weekend still buoys me to this day.

Over and over again, the name Julian of Norwich came up in the spaces I was finding myself in, whether on a page or off of lips. So finally, about a year into my venture, I picked up her writings for myself. From the very start, I felt a connection with her words. By the time she used the word *Mother* for God I was basically screaming. *Where had this theology been all my life? Why had it been kept from me? Did anyone else realize what this meant?!* I felt like Elizabeth when the infant John the Baptist kicked in her womb at the sound of Mary's voice. The joy and relief were palpable in my body.

*   *   *

"As truly as God is our Father, just as truly is God our Mother."

"This beautiful word 'mother' is so sweet and kind in itself that it cannot be attributed to anyone but God. Only he who is our true Mother and source of all life may rightfully be called by this name."

"I realized that the Second Person [of the Trinity] is really our Mother. This beloved being works with us as a parent here on earth. We were created with a twofold soul, sensual and spiritual. Our spiritual essence is with God-the-Father. Our sensual nature lies with the Second Person of the Trinity, God-the-Mother, in whom we are rooted by virtue of our creation. In taking on our flesh, the Second Person became our Mother of Mercy."

* * *

To Julian of Norwich, feminine depictions of God were not radical, subversive, or rebellious. They were obvious, inevitable, and clear. She didn't feel the need to defend her words, she simply wrote what was revealed to her in the visions: God has masculine qualities and God has feminine qualities. Both are important. *Voilà!*

Unfortunately, it's not so easy for most of us. We are constantly filtering our theology through what we consider to be permissible. Unlike Dame Julian, we tend to defer to precedent rather than follow the nudgings of our own souls. We trust those in authority more than we trust ourselves.

But the witness of Julian of Norwich asks us to be brave; to dig deep within and experience God in our guts, not just in our churches; to engage our spiritual imaginations in the pursuit of a salvation that sets us free *today*—not just after death.

Humans don't like change. That's no big secret. And the very idea of changing how we approach God can feel scary. So I think it's important to remember that this is not an either/or kind of deal. We don't have to forfeit the image of Father for God if that has brought comfort to our hearts. But we do have to make room for something else, too.

Amplifying the parts of God that women can see ourselves in does not mean we can't also uphold the parts that are more traditionally masculine. The key is balance. And yet to achieve that balance, the ones currently holding the power must necessarily lose some of that power—and that's where things get sticky. It turns out, humans really don't enjoy losing power. But you know who spoke a lot about the necessity of forfeiting power? Jesus. So, yeah, maybe we need to sit on that one a bit.

You know something else that Jesus said? He said he was like a mother hen longing to gather her baby chicks under her wings. His love for the people of Israel could only be described as maternal. (*Duh,* Julian of Norwich would say.)

But this is far from the only biblical nod to the divine feminine. The entire representation of Wisdom in the book of Proverbs is female. In Isaiah 66:13 the prophet tells us that God declares, "As a mother comforts her child, so will I comfort you" (NSV). Earlier in the same book, God describes crying out like a woman in labor, gasping and panting. We are so accustomed to skimming over these metaphors that we don't stop and really contemplate them.

When you prayerfully imagine God comforting you like a mother, it should be specific. What does God look like in that moment? What do you feel? How do you experience this differently than when you pray with passages about God as Father? Neither is better or worse than the other, but we are lying to ourselves if we say they are not different.

Likewise, if you try to pray with the imagery of God in birthing labor but all you can imagine is a male God, well, that meditation is going to come to a screeching halt. Childbirth is one of the most sacred acts that we humans engage in; and not only are biologically male bodies incapable of it but for most of human history it was done without men anywhere in the vicinity. Certainly at the time of Isaiah's writing, no man in Israel was following the midwives into the delivery tent.

Sure, these days plenty of good men have been active partners in support of the coming of their babies. But would you rather be told about the experience from one of them or from the women who moved tiny human beings through and out of their very own bodies?

Yeah, that's what I thought.

Once, during a homily in a Mass I was attending, an earnest young priest likened the Eucharist to a breastfeeding mother (in theory, not one in the pews) saying, "This is my body, broken for you. Take and eat." As a breastfeeding mom myself, I appreciated that. It was nice to have that connection acknowledged. It was noteworthy. But it didn't take my breath away.

Do you know what *has* taken my breath away? Visiting a friend four days postpartum when she is still wearing the disposable hospital panties to catch her blood, when her breasts have swollen into rock-hard melons, when her nipples are cracked and bleeding, when her baby begins crying because he is hungry and she begins crying because she dreads the pain that is to come while he finds his latch, when her eyes meet mine and silently tell me she cannot, will not do this one more time, and I tuck her hair behind her ear and stroke her baby's downy head and tell her, *You are the strongest creature who has ever lived. You are made of stars.* Then she puts her baby to her nipple yet again and winces in pain, shoulders tight; then she looks at the child who came out of her body and the hurt melts away and every pore on her face is shining with glory and the tiniest hint of a smile flickers when she says, *This is my body, broken for you. Take and eat.*

There are things of God only a woman knows.

You are *invited* to imagine a feminine face of God; not only is it permissible but it is beneficial. You will encounter the divine in entirely new ways, from fresh and exciting angles, receiving inspiration and understanding to help you see in places you might have gotten stuck.

Engaging with the feminine face of God does not mean

obliterating the masculine one. Not only is there room for both in our spiritual imaginations but Julian of Norwich would argue that there's room for both *at the same time*. Dame Julian approached gender binaries playfully, with a refreshing absence of precision. She repeatedly wrote things like "Jesus births," "he mothers," and "Jesus as both Son and Mother," knowing in full confidence that the One who whispered the world into existence does not conform to gender binaries established by human society. The divine transcends our language and social constructs. Perhaps God's most appropriate pronouns are they/them.

In the midst of our own discomfort and hesitancies, Julian of Norwich offers an ease, a gentle reassurance, that God is much larger than our finite brains can comprehend. This God we know and love—this God we have experienced—is big enough to hold it all. The question is, can we put aside our fears and prejudices and get on board with that?

Spiritual practices or beliefs that come from the East, Africa, or Indigenous Western cultures are too often viewed with skepticism, avoidance, or (in extreme cases) claims of the demonic. Human instinct is to stick to what we know, stick to what is "like us," stick to a sense of felt safety. That's natural, sure. But it doesn't help us grow. It doesn't leave much room for the Spirit to do a new thing in us. Responding instead to new ideas with curiosity and sincere questions helps us discern what to pick up and bring along on our journey, and what to respectfully leave behind.

There is no need to fear, for "the mystery of the feminine is not a fearsome mystery," writes Leonardo Boff in *The Maternal Face of God*. "It is a mystery of intimacy and tenderness. And it is far more of a mystery than a problem. Problems have solutions. Once solved, they are gone for good. But mystery has no solutions."

* * *

What if incorporating the divine feminine just doesn't do it for you? Cool, no problem. There's a universe full of symbols and metaphors for God, and they will not all speak to each one of us in equal measure. Many of us find ourselves gravitating to different "faces" of God at different times in our life spans, changing like the seasons, depending on our circumstances, wounds, needs, or prayer habits.

And yet. (Were you waiting for that?) Incorporating the feminine realities of God into our collective spiritual experiences is a justice issue. We're not talking about whether you want to hang a "Jesus as the Good Shepherd" painting in your sanctuary, we're talking about whether we are freeing ourselves from centuries of oppression and marginalization of women. Every metaphor is not created equal.

And for the record, it's not only women who need freedom from the claws of patriarchy: men do, too. For it has been an equally cruel system for them, cultivating a fertile field for toxic masculinity, insecurity, hierarchy, homophobia, and emotional repression, among other problems. Every human person is composed of both masculine and feminine qualities, and when we suppress one in favor of the other, we have unhealthy individuals and an unhealthy society. It's time for balance and equality. It's time for liberation for all people.

Such liberation is already under way. The Spirit is already doing a new thing in the world, and is doing so with a feminine face. It is our choice, then, whether to participate with the Spirit's movement or to resist it.

"The blessed wound of our Beloved is open, eager to heal

us," writes Julian of Norwich. "The sweet and gracious hands of our Mother are already encircling us, diligent and soothing." For the sake of all our healing, may we not miss out.

Questions for Prayer and Reflection

1. When you think about engaging with God in the feminine, what feels hopeful to you? What feels uncomfortable?
2. What has been your experience as a woman in religious or spiritual spaces? Have you ever noticed the prevalence of the masculine at the expense of the feminine? Do spaces where this occurs feel safe to you?
3. How might your personal life of contemplation benefit from incorporating the divine feminine into your spirituality? What parts of God might be activated in your soul?

CHAPTER EIGHT

Wherein Sin and Hell
Lose a Whole Lot of Power

The colors and sounds of the streets of Juárez infiltrated my senses, spinning my head with foreignness that smelled a bit like fear. I lingered on the outer edge of our group as the sound crew readied the microphones. At the appointed time, the group leader grabbed a mic, stepped with confidence into the open square, and began to preach in broken Spanish.

When I had signed up for the college ministry's spring break mission trip, I had done so because I longed for friends, not because I wanted to evangelize the people of Mexico. Just a few weeks prior, I had been nursing my broken heart and repressed trauma when a kind, funny girl with curly hair introduced herself in a coffee shop. I was thrilled when she invited me to her church's small group after just a few minutes of chatting and surprised but pleased when she suggested that I come on their spring break trip as well. It was a light at the end of my dark tunnel of isolation; for the first time in over a year, I felt a twinge of hope. Maybe I wouldn't be alone anymore.

I was raised in the kind of church where a mission trip meant you went to Appalachia and painted debilitated houses. But this new church played hardball. At the mission trip orientation I learned we would not be wielding paintbrushes; we would be wielding Bibles. After all, the eternal salvation of souls was on the line; there was no time to mess around. This trip was all about street evangelism, which did not appeal to my sensibilities, but I didn't want to forfeit my newfound friendships, and who knew? Maybe it wouldn't be as intense as it sounded.

It was every bit as intense as it sounded.

Doing my best to ignore the growing knot in my stomach, I tried to decipher what our esteemed street preacher was saying to the masses of brown-skinned people who seemed accustomed to seeing random Americans pop over the border to do odd things in their city center. I didn't speak Spanish, but based on the rather extensive training we were given beforehand, I assumed it was probably "the bridge."

The bridge is a model of evangelism that explains salvation like this: God is on one cliff and you are on a different cliff, separated by a large void caused by your sin. You can't reach God because of your sin, and God apparently can't reach you either, so you need a bridge to reach across the divide: Jesus.

There are about a million theological questions raised by this model, and anyone with much experience with other religions or even other strands of Christian thought would be wise to probe it, but when you're twenty years old and just looking for a concrete truth to believe in, it makes a lot of sense. So, despite the fact that it made me anxious and uncomfortable, I accepted that our team's duty was to share the bridge with as many people as possible in five days.

I had not yet learned to listen to the feeling in my gut that said this wasn't for me. I had not yet learned to trust myself above authority figures. But I *had* encountered God in a mystical way over the course of a month about a year before. In a rock-bottom moment of my life, the comfort and peace of the Scriptures had come alive to me. The presence of whoever Jesus was felt real and deeply personal. I had experienced unexplainable hope and joy. I knew what the Spirit felt like in my body.

Talking to strangers about sin and hell did not feel like that, even though the conversations were punctuated with assurances of unconditional divine love. It didn't add up. It made me feel uncomfortable and tense in my body. It felt forced and filled with dread. But I was told it was the most loving thing to do.

It didn't matter how hard it was if people were being saved from hell.

* * *

If you think about it, hell is one of the strangest theological points that humans could fixate on. It is impossible for anyone to reliably report on what happens after we die or how the afterlife is ordered, and the Bible spends exponentially more time on issues of justice and liberation on earth than it does on what happens after death. Theologians have debated the topic for centuries, with no definitive conclusions—because definitive conclusions on the topic will always elude us. And yet, for many of our religious spaces, hell has become the singular issue, the nexus around which all else moves.

Of course it makes sense for humanity to wrestle with death and the terror of not knowing what comes afterward. When the human mind can organize around black-and-white thinking, it feels safe. It's our primal brain seeking to meet one of our most basic needs.

Consider our ancestors. If they were being hunted by a wild animal, there was no room for nuance. They weren't empathizing with the hungry beast while running for their lives. Their brains were signaling, *Beast: bad. Staying alive: good.* No shades of gray in sight.

In the same way, separating people as *good and evil, us and them, saved and unsaved* feels good to our primal brains. Holding to a certainty about the distinction between heaven and hell—and knowing exactly the rules surrounding them—plays directly to our survival instincts. But does it offer us an intimate, emotionally safe, and tender relationship with God? Does it move us closer to a life marked by trust and hope? Does it help us love our neighbor *in a way that feels like love to them*?

It's true that many of our beloved mystics had visions of hell. But it's also true that they interpreted those visions in a wide variety of ways; some, like Thérèse of Lisieux, even reached the conclusion that hell exists but is empty.

Our girl Julian of Norwich had some spine-tingling visions of hell herself. In her fourth showing, the anchoress witnesses the blood of Christ descend into hell, where it "bursts forth her bonds," before covering the earth and ascending to heaven. There, the blood "flows throughout heaven enjoying the salvation of all humankind that are and shall be."

Later, she admits to struggling with the tension between what she witnessed in her private revelations and what the institutional Church had taught her about hell. "All these [heathens] may be condemned to hell without end, for so holy Church teaches me to believe. And thinking about this, I thought it was impossible that all manner of things should be well as our Lord showed me," she writes, reflecting on the promise that Jesus had spoken in an earlier vision. "I had no answer from our Lord but this: 'What is impossible to you, is not impossible to me. I shall keep my word in all things, and I shall make all things well.'"

Now that's a word that feels good, true, and beautiful to the deepest core of the body and soul.

Once, in one of her earliest visions, Dame Julian was shown

a tiny round ball that looked like a hazelnut. When she spent time contemplating what it could possibly represent, the answer came as if from both within and outside of her: "This is all that is made. . . . This lasts and it will go on lasting forever because God loves it. And so it is with every being that God loves."

What if we chose to see as a mystic—for each of us has a mystic within us, waiting to be unlocked—and meditate on the hazelnut? To the One who exists outside of time and space, this tiny nut contains everything that has ever been made. Let yourself try to fathom that for a moment: not just human history, not just an earth that is billions of years old, not just our galaxy, but each and every galaxy and all of their molecules since the beginning of whatever is our minuscule construct of time. It's all there, in the hazelnut. And it will go on lasting forever "because God loves it."

What if it were as simple as that? What if love were as powerful as that? Why not believe that it could be?

*   *   *

Exactly a decade after my attempt at evangelizing the streets of Juárez, I was confirmed in the Catholic Church. Many things went into that decision—my discovery and embrace of Catholic social teaching being a big one—but the attractiveness of the very different approach to hell was pretty high on the list. After years of doing missions with an evangelical church, I had eventually left behind the rigidity of a teaching on salvation that assumed eternal damnation of people who didn't speak, look, or worship like me. I was done.

The ambiguity of the Catholic teaching on the afterlife pleased me. No one was holding hell over people's heads to scare them into crossing some imaginary salvation line. In fact, hell was hardly mentioned; jokes about shaving time off purgatory by refraining from flipping off another driver or cleaning up your kid's vomit were much more common. Purgatory was a foreign concept to me, and my feelings surrounding it were ambivalent, but there was something nice about a collective acknowledgment that the world is not black and white. Purgatory—whatever it is and whether it even exists—is like a giant admission that we humans don't actually know the mind of God.

Since the Catholic sensibility about salvation is that it is a constant conversion process spanning one's entire life, I found there was less pressure to "save souls" and more room to practice solidarity and accompaniment. The theology surrounding the afterlife was wide and vague enough for an entire range of beliefs, and it was a comfort to me to feel like I wasn't committing to one singular way of thinking for life. Catholicism felt large enough to hold all of my future spiritual evolution, whatever it might be.

I'm happy to report that nearly a decade—and quite a bit of spiritual evolution—later, I have found that to be true. But another thing I have found is that Catholics are not actually less fearful than Protestants; they are simply afraid of different things.

Catholics, I learned, tend to have a much more scrupulous approach to sin than I had experienced in any of my previous faith communities. The sacrament of reconciliation (a.k.a. going to confession) is a beautiful, ancient practice with a good deal of spiritual benefit when done rightly. But the risk is that it can be held too tight, depended on too fearfully, and it can damage one's perception of God. This isn't always the case, naturally, but it's something my unique perspective enabled me to observe as an adult convert.

Of course, you don't have to be Catholic to find yourself fixated on your own sin. If you're not a particularly religious person, you might not ever think of that word. The literal definition of sin is "to miss the mark," and all humans share that experience—as well as the spiral of emotions that come along with it. Perhaps for you it's a nagging feeling of unworthiness or being unlovable. Perhaps it feels like shame or insecurity. Perhaps sin convinces us that we have sabotaged our lives, destroyed something holy, or inflicted a harm that will last forever. To this, Julian of Norwich has to say, "I shall do nothing but sin, yet my sin will not prevent the work of goodness."

We give sin too much power, and it has only the power we give it. So maybe let's stop adding fuel to the fire. Mama Julian is telling us that our mistakes, our missing the mark, are not the end of the world; they won't prevent the work of goodness or the movement of the Spirit. Can we do better? Yes. And we will. But nothing prevents a person from doing better quite like believing they are the scum of the earth.

Are you questioning my authority to say that sin has only the power we give it? Fair enough. But if you don't want to hear it from me, hear it from Julian of Norwich. Over and over again through the course of her showings, she confesses to not being able to find sin anywhere. This perplexes her for a while, for where was the weight of this Super Important Doctrine that she had been taught all her life? If she was going to be a legitimate mystic with visions of Jesus, where was her message of hellfire and brimstone? Where were the warnings, the ominous urgings to repent?

"In all this sin was never shown," she writes, simple and re-petitive, countless times.

Eventually, she comes to this conclusion: "But all this while, I never once saw sin. For I believe it has neither manner of sub-stance nor part of being, and it would not even be known save for the pain it causes. Yet this pain is indeed something, as I see it; for it purges and makes us know ourself as we ask for mercy."

Sin doesn't have substance or being, Julian says. It is nothing. Powerless. The only way we even know it exists is the pain it causes—and, oofta, there can be pain. There can be serious, serious pain. But even in that, the Dame has good news. Suffering does two things: it helps us know ourselves in raw self-honesty, and it stirs our hearts to reach for mercy. In short? It fills life with tenderness.

It is this tenderness of the divine that echoes through Julian of Norwich when she utters her famous words "All shall be well." But I am not content to give you the CliffsNotes version. You need to hear it all in context. Rarely have more stunning spiritual words been written.

" 'It is true that sin is the cause of all this pain, but all shall be well, and all shall be well, and all manner of thing shall be well.' This was said so tenderly, without blame of any kind toward me or to anybody else. Therefore it would be a great unkindness to wonder or complain of sin to God, since he puts no blame on me."

May we live our days leaning into the breast of divine tenderness, knowing that all shall be well, and all shall be well, and all manner of thing shall be well.

*   *   *

We are each presented with a choice to make: what will be the hinge post of our relationship with and beliefs about That Which We Call God? Will it be fear of punishment—whether temporal or eternal? Or will it be love?

As for me? I have decided to leave the theological debates about sin and hell to those who care to have them. I am placing my bets on the side of love.

But it's not a shallow, wishy-washy way of having faith: my conviction that divine love is the most powerful force in the universe is rooted in Scripture and Tradition. But equally important to me, it is rooted in my own experience.

Franciscan friar Father Richard Rohr describes faith as a tricycle: Scripture, Tradition, and Experience. Leave off any one of the three and the ego takes control. Rohr writes, "Christians who say 'only Scripture' end up being unconsciously dishonest and inconsistent, because they are relying on their own 'tradition' of interpreting those Scriptures (without acknowledging it). Even more importantly, we must recognize that we cannot *not* rely upon our own experience. There is no such thing as a completely unbiased opinion! Since we all use tradition and experience anyway, why not admit it and thereby hold ourselves accountable?"

This explanation made sense to me and also validated the very real role that my experience with God plays in my personal belief system. I realize that I am privileged to have come this far in life without unbearable pain and suffering, and I recognize that this good fortune has formed my perception of God as warm and loving. That conclusion is more difficult to reach for those who have had harder lives.

But I do believe with every atom of my being that such a relationship with God is possible for everyone who wants it. It might take a lot of therapy to get there. It might mean leaving certain religious traditions or churches and finding more nourishing ones. It might mean making major life changes. But it also might just mean closing the bedroom door, sitting down on the floor, and waiting to feel loved. It might be as simple as that.

The point of the whole faith thing is union, and you were made for union. Yes, you, who feel like the least mystical person on earth. Yes, you, who has a hard time sitting still. (Pro tip from someone with ADHD: take meditative hikes instead.) You were made for union with Love Itself.

Julian of Norwich called it "one-ing," or being "one-d" to God. Isn't that lovely? Sign me up for that kind of spirituality, please and thanks.

In the introduction of her translation of *The Showings of Julian of Norwich,* Mirabai Starr writes, "Sin is nothing but separation from our divine source. And separation from the Holy One is nothing but illusion. We are always and forever connected in love with our Beloved. Therefore, sin is not real; only love is real. Julian did not require a Divinity degree to arrive at this conclusion. . . . the Holy One . . . assured her that he had loved her since before he made her and would love her till the end of time. And it is with this great love, he revealed, that he loves all beings. Our only task is to remember this and rejoice."

Questions for Prayer and Reflection

1. Reflect on your own religious history with sin and hell from an early age until now. What were the messages that were formed in you?
2. How do Julian of Norwich's words about sin and hell sit with you?
3. Consider the three parts of the "faith tricycle." Are there wheels that you have ignored in favor of others? Is there an invitation for something new there?

THÉRÈSE OF LISIEUX

CHAPTER NINE

Subversive Insignificance in a World Hungry for Fame

"Grow your followers by 10k in minutes!"
"Take your small business to the next level!"
"Increase your website traffic with these SEO tips!"
"Make a six-figure salary as an influencer!"
"Sell more books by doing less work!"
"Create and market a course in 7 days!"

We are living in an unprecedented—and frankly, rather weird—time in history. We are the first generation to have the internet, adapting virtually overnight to accessing all the information in the world at our fingertips. And now we're the first generation to navigate social media, which often feels like the internet on steroids, meth, weed, and LSD all at the same time. It gets crazy up in here.

Social media is still a new field of research, but the science is already speaking loud and clear. Study after study confirms the impact social media has on our brains, from what we decide to purchase, to whether we deem a piece of news trustworthy, to the beliefs we hold about our own self-worth. We have all heard the harrowing statistics about the dopamine released in our brains with every like, share, comment, or retweet—and how the pattern of social media addiction mimics that found in substance abuse.

The conversation surrounding social media consumption is pretty well documented, but there is far less being said about the mental and emotional effects of social media as a business tool, especially for the self-employed, and *especially* for women.

In some ways, the explosion of social media in our generation has granted women extraordinary new freedoms to reimagine work-and-home life balance. Many women have been able to stay at home with their children while running a small business, writing a book, selling their art, teaching a course, getting paid to advertise products they like, or any number of other great things. My husband recently received anti-racism training from a Black homeschooling mom of two whom he found through the glories of social media. The fact that doors are opening for more women is cause for celebration.

And yet, the whole "bring home the bacon while staying at home" thing is not a workable reality for most women. Most women are unlikely to have the skill sets, or the mental or emotional capacity, or the marketing savvy, or the money to get started, or one of a million other necessities to have a successful (or even just enjoyable) side gig or income source. The sad truth of our society is that no, most women cannot have it all. And even those who appear to usually tell a different story if you ask them in private.

If it were as simple as it sounds, we could all accept that this path is right for some women and not for others; we could easily see which side of the line we're meant to stand on, and we could move forward with our lives in joy and peace. But the problem is, it doesn't always feel so simple. It often feels very confusing.

Many women feel pressured to have an entrepreneurial pursuit, even if they don't need the money. Moms—especially moms of young children who spend much of their days in the home— often feel overlooked or invisible, and the allure of establishing an identity separate from motherhood can be really strong. But instead of getting curious and discerning what we need *(A hobby? A class? A part-time job? A night out with friends?)*, we just look down at the thing most relied upon to greet us with stimulation: the phone. And then we compare ourselves to what we see there.

When we spend a significant portion of our days watching people like us carve out niches for themselves, whether from redecorating their houses or leading an exercise regimen in the cutest new Lululemon ensemble, it's understandable that we would become convinced that wielding some kind of "influence" is necessary for a happy life. And once you get your feet wet, heaven help you: the pressure to grow, expand, and produce can become a roller coaster that never stops.

We are a society quickly losing touch with the worthiness of the small. We are buying into the falsehood that size is the only valid measurement of our work. In a day and age where everybody worships the "influencer," it is becoming increasingly difficult to simply be a person who does what you love because it brings you joy—and, hey, maybe it brings a few other people joy, too.

There is problem enough in that quantitative approach to work, but it doesn't end there; our work always comes back to our sense of self. Done with integrity and discipline, meaningful work can strengthen our self-respect and self-trust. But when our work is punctuated by intrusive thoughts about sales numbers, follower counts, and post engagements, both the work and our souls feel compromised. We begin to doubt ourselves, doubt our abilities, doubt the joy we once took in what we do. Slowly, we move toward self-abandonment. And self-abandonment always feels like separation from God.

Around one hundred and thirty years ago, a young woman lived who could never imagine the technological thread that weaves our social landscape today. And yet she is exactly the one prepared to help us know what to do with it.

*   *   *

Thérèse Martin was born in Normandy, France, in 1873 to Louis and Zélie Martin, devout Catholics who had each separately tried to enter religious life and was denied before marrying each other. Thérèse was the last of five living Martin children, though the family also birthed and lost four others, and as the youngest, she enjoyed the privileged position of being doted on by all.

Louis and Zélie ordered their family's rhythm in keeping with their own religious fervor. The Martins could reliably be found attending daily Mass, engaging in formal family prayer, making pilgrimages and retreats, and fasting according to the liturgical calendar; and their faith was not without works. The mother and father prioritized the works of mercy and taught their children to respectfully care for the poor. All in all, the Martin family was a happy one, spearheaded by parents who both sincerely enjoyed being parents.

But life was not all idyllic. Long before Thérèse was born, Zélie discovered a large lump in her breast that caused her grave concern—a concern her male doctors waved off as unfounded and hysterical. Zélie became sicker and sicker with breast cancer. All in all, she suffered for eleven years. She passed away when her youngest daughter was just four and a half years old.

Later, Thérèse would remember a striking amount of detail from the tragedy: the last rites being administered, the words of her grieving father, the size of her mother's coffin. She recalls the decade between her mother's death and her entering the convent as a young teenager as having been the most painful time of her life, noting that her happy disposition changed dramatically after the loss.

Yet she also speaks of being surrounded by tenderness—the tenderness of both God and loved ones, especially after her father moved the family to Lisieux to be nearer to their mother's sister. For his part, Louis became even closer to the children after his wife's death, and Thérèse recounts plenty of precious memories of playing and adventuring with her beloved papa.

By the time she was fourteen, Thérèse had witnessed two older sisters enter the Carmelite convent and had determined to follow in their footsteps, much to the grief of her father, who hoped his "little queen" would stay near him. Thérèse became a postulant in 1888, a novice in 1889, and took her final vows, becoming a full-fledged nun of the Carmelite order, in 1890. She died of tuberculosis in 1897 at just twenty-four years old.

Okay, someone has to say it: all in all, Thérèse of Lisieux led a remarkably unremarkable life. So why are we still talking about her?

Thérèse wrote down her life's story, not because she believed it to be important or even noteworthy but because, like all writers, she felt she had something to say and deserved to say it. Her account is now published under the title *Story of a Soul* and has been read by millions of people worldwide. Thérèse never intended her writing to be for public distribution, only for the eyes of her Martin sisters and the Mother Prioress at the convent. But, it turned out, fate would have it differently.

In nineteenth-century Europe, belief in a punitive God who demanded perfection permeated the religious imagination. And yet this was a far cry from Thérèse's experience. She instead expressed a revelation of the kindness, tenderness, and unconditional love of God—a God who wants us to come near like weak and needy children, not like flawless victors; a God who doesn't need us to make an impact but wants us for relationship.

This way of approaching God was so countercultural for its time that despite its clear gospel origins, Thérèse thought it was brand new—and indeed it was, for many readers. She called it "the little way." Unlike the grandiose spiritual power plays that elicit public admiration, the little way of Thérèse of Lisieux is small, humble, and content to be so. It rejects the pressure to perform and produce, and instead rests in the "enoughness" of being human and finding rest in the arms of divine love. It is childlike in its trusting abandonment and absence of striving.

It is this love, and only this love, that matters, Thérèse would say. So convinced was she of the intricacies of such love that she called it a science.

"The science of Love, ah, yes, this word resounds sweetly in the ear of my soul, and I desire only this science," she wrote. "I understand so well . . . that this love is the only good I ambition."

*   *   *

A decade ago, I was on the prowl. Catholics have a tradition of choosing a canonized saint to be taken as a patron on the day of our confirmation—which, for most Catholics, happens in the notoriously flaky teen years, but as a thirty-year-old convert I was taking it much more seriously. Determined to find the strongest, most subversive female to take as my patron saint, I left no stone unturned in the hunt for whichever one would make me look the most hard-core.

My favorite historical Catholic figure was Dorothy Day, a radical socialist, anarchist, frequently imprisoned war protester, founder of the Catholic Worker movement, and all-around bad-ass. But she wasn't an official saint yet, so I had to find a Plan B. In her own extensive writings, Day sang the praises of someone named Saint Thérèse of Lisieux, so I figured I would probably like her, too. It was as good a place to start as any.

But, oh. When I started reading *Story of a Soul,* I'm pretty sure my nose wrinkled up before I got past the second page. This Thérèse person was exactly the kind of pious, fragile little thing that Christianity loves to uphold as the quintessential woman, the kind of woman who will automatically be called a saint based on demure personality alone, no matter what she does with her life. Why on earth did Dorothy Day adore her? I couldn't see it, and I'm still not entirely sure what made me keep reading.

But I did keep reading. And along the way, I was surprised at the contradictions this woman contained. (Yet isn't this the truth about every woman?) Thérèse really was as syrupy sweet as she seems at first glance, *and* that sweetness does not negate the fact that she also had dreams and desires that were bold, courageous, and, yes, even downright subversive.

Of a pilgrimage to Rome, she wrote, "I still cannot understand why women are so easily excommunicated in Italy, for every minute someone was saying, 'Don't enter here! Don't enter there, you will be excommunicated!' Ah! Poor women, how they are misunderstood! And yet they love God in much larger numbers than men do and during the Passion of Our Lord, women had more courage than the apostles."

Where is the lie, Thérèse, my girl? Where is the lie?

Thérèse of Lisieux was a woman who deeply desired to make an impact on the world. She was not satisfied with loving her family members and, later, her religious sisters; she longed to be out in the world, caring for the broken and spreading the good news of love and mercy. She actually dreamed of being martyred, so intense was her passion, and even fantasized about what kind of death she would undergo when she was hypothetically killed for love of God and humanity.

When Thérèse eventually came to accept that her life would be cut short by sickness, she consoled herself by deciding to spend all of eternity ministering to those on earth who were in need. She wrote, "If God answers my requests, my heaven will be spent on earth up until the end of the world. Yes, I want to spend my heaven in doing good on earth."

She did not shrug and give up on affecting the world when she realized circumstances would limit her; she opened her own damn window in the face of a closed door.

But it wasn't just a life of missions and service that attracted Thérèse: her hunger was extensive and insatiable. "To be Your *Spouse,* to be a *Carmelite,* and by my union with You to be the *Mother* of souls, should not this suffice me? . . . And yet I feel within me other *vocations.* I feel the vocation of the WARRIOR, THE PRIEST, THE APOSTLE, THE DOCTOR, THE MARTYR." This chick was a feminist if ever there was one.

To admit to a calling to be a priest is a controversial taboo in the Catholic Church, even now! And yet Thérèse was unashamed and certain, even while knowing the fulfillment of her dream would be impossible. Still, she dreamed. "I feel in me the vocation of the PRIEST," she writes as a twenty-something female in the 1800s. "With what love, O Jesus, I would carry You in my hands when, at my voice, You would come down from heaven. And with what love I would give you to souls!"

In 2021, *The New Yorker* ran a feature entitled "The Women

Who Want to Be Priests," covering the increasingly vocal movement of women pushing for equal clerical rights in the Roman
Catholic Church. The article pointed to Thérèse of Lisieux as
historical precedent for this felt call, noting:

> Thérèse's sisters had given testimony at her beatification
> proceedings that she had asked them to shave the top of
> her head so that she would have a tonsure—an emblem
> of priestly devotion. Thérèse had written in her diary, "I
> feel in me the vocation of a Priest," and she had declared
> that she would die at the age of twenty-four, because that is
> the age at which she would have been ordained—and God
> would surely spare her the pain of not being able to exercise
> her calling. Thérèse died at twenty-four, of tuberculosis.

In honor of the validity of her calling, the Women's Ordination
Conference, one of my favorite faith-based advocacy groups, has
dubbed Thérèse of Lisieux the patron saint of women's ordination.
    In 2014 she also became my patron saint, which still reminds
me not to judge people without getting to know them first. While
I'll defend the boldness of her desires to the ground, ultimately
it wasn't our similarities that made the strongest impression on
me, but rather our differences. Thérèse has always been able to
find the specific places in my ego that need prodding and sneak
in to give them a good poke.
    Now, do I have times when I read an isolated quote by her
and fear my eyes might roll straight out of their sockets? Gentle
reader, yes I do. There is an element of sweetness and innocence
to her that my saucy self will never find palatable. But I need
Thérèse of Lisieux in my life. I need her to remind me that my

worth is not tied to my impact; that small acts of love are more powerful than sales numbers or social media followers; that the interior life will always matter more than the exterior.

I need her to teach me to stop and smell the flowers.

*   *   *

I was one of those stereotypical little girls who was already dreaming of becoming a mommy by the time I started elementary school—maybe not the most radical feminist thing to admit, but true nonetheless. By the time eighth grade rolled around, I already had the name of my future daughter picked out: Daisy. (No, I didn't end up using it when I finally had a daughter two decades later, but that's not the point of this story.)

I'm not sure what it was about daisies that attracted me. Maybe it was because it was the nineties and Drew Barrymore was wearing them in her hair on every page of *Us Weekly*. Maybe it was because Meg Ryan had dubbed them "the friendliest flower" in *You've Got Mail*. Maybe it was because bell-bottoms had come back to the runways. Whatever the reason, I could legitimately feel the serotonin releasing in my brain anytime I saw the white petals of a daisy. So, like any teen girl would, I decorated my entire bedroom with them—the crowning glory of which was an inflatable chair that was too uncomfortable to actually sit on but sure did look cute.

Trends aside, I'm still curious about why I loved that particular flower so much that I would reserve its name for my hypothetical future progeny. I have a hunch that the daisy somehow represented my evolving pubescent understanding of myself. Like a daisy, I was lovely but not stunning, cheerful but not attention seeking, wild and free but not ambitious. There were plenty of flowers that I could acknowledge were more glamorous or ornate, but they weren't my favorites. Maybe because they weren't me.

As a little girl, Thérèse of Lisieux loved flowers, too. She recalls spending blissful days tending blossoms in the garden her father had given her, picking the most beautiful ones by the stems and arranging them as an altar against the garden wall. Joining the Carmelite order later required that she give up the freedom to frolic through fields of wildflowers, and flowers were such a joy to her soul that Thérèse felt the grief of this loss deeply. So she found it that much sweeter when, upon taking her vows, she was overwhelmed with more flowers delivered to her than she had ever seen in one place—cornflowers, daisies, poppies, and even corn cockles, a certain wildflower from her childhood that she hadn't seen since moving to Lisieux after her mother's death. She felt deeply seen by God; she had not been overlooked by her divine Beloved after all.

As time went on, Thérèse's passion for flowers evolved into a revelation that she couldn't help but explain to anyone who would listen. She called herself "the little flower." (And again, I just have to say: Thérèse, you are not helping your nauseatingly sweet reputation here.) It sounds juvenile, but actually the theology—which she said God revealed to her through "the book of nature"—is quite moving.

Thérèse writes:

I understood how all the flowers God has created are beautiful, how the splendor of the rose and the whiteness of the lily do not take away the perfume of the little violet or the delightful simplicity of the daisy. I understood that if all flowers wanted to be roses, nature would lose her springtime beauty, and the fields would no longer be decked out with little wild flowers. And so it is in the world of souls.

If we could internalize this truth, what would happen to our sense of self? What would become of our proclivity to compare ourselves with others, to compete for influence or impact? If we could identify the "flower" that is us and settle into all the unique gifts, beauty, and quirks that come with being that particular flower, would we be happier? More content? More supportive of others? What would happen to our scarcity mindset?

The little flower continues:

> Just as the sun shines simultaneously on the tall cedars and on each little flower as though it were alone on the earth, so Our Lord is occupied particularly with each soul as though there were no others like it. And just as in nature all the seasons are arranged in such a way as to make the humblest daisy bloom on a set day, in the same way, everything works out for the good of each soul.

There is great freedom in deciding to love yourself exactly as you are; even greater freedom in believing deep in your bones that you are seen, nurtured, adored, and will be forever taken care of by the Holy One. These are the kinds of freedoms that release us from an obsession with things like platform and impact. These freedoms allow us to hold any influence we have loosely, stewarding it well, but knowing it can be gone in the blink of an eye and life would still be beautiful. We would still be worthy.

Thérèse of Lisieux might just be the anti-influencer; not because she had no impact—clearly, she did; and not because she never wanted it—but because she ultimately came to a place of internal freedom that didn't *need* it.

The biggest influence that Thérèse had on the world came, ironically, from proclaiming to us that influence doesn't matter.

That the success or failure of someone else doesn't matter. Hell, that your own success or failure doesn't matter. For in the end, it's all about love, she would say: loving yourself, letting God love you, and letting that love direct itself back to God. And this small, nearly imperceptible cycle of love makes for the most breathtaking bouquet of flowers.

Questions for Prayer and Reflection

1. What observations do you have about "influencer culture" at large? How have you noticed it affecting you personally?
2. Thérèse of Lisieux wrote, "Love is the only good ambition." How does this statement find integration with ambitions you have—professional, economic, a bucket list, et cetera?
3. If you were a flower, which one would you be? How do you feel about that flower? How does it compare with other flowers? How do you learn to love that flower instead of envying another?

CHAPTER TEN

Nursing the Mother Wound

From a wall in my home office, Mary watches over me in more than a dozen ways. She is Native; she is Black; she is a Latina immigrant; she is white and plump, young and pixie-like, pregnant, breastfeeding, crowned, curled into a flower, or pierced by seven swords. Each portrait is unique, part of a carefully curated collection that grows bigger every year. I delight in finding new ways to imagine her, delight in finding more and more artists who feel compelled to show us the particular version of Mary that they know and love.

But my favorites among all of my Marys tend to be the ones who look, shall we say, *a little intense*. The ones with lifted chins, squared shoulders, and certain eyes. The kind of art that men on Twitter grumble over and criticize for not seeming "maternal" enough.

Well, I have news for Todd on Twitter: for me, there is nothing more maternal than Mary as protectress; nothing that makes me feel safer or more nurtured than a Queen who stares straight ahead with a baby in her arms and a "fuck around and find out" look on her face. (Apologies to the pearls that are being clutched right now.)

Because it's *hard* to be a woman in this world. It's hard to walk through life with the intergenerational trauma of unsafety pulsing through our nervous systems. Every single woman whose DNA we carry has, to some degree, shouldered the burden of danger: physical danger that puts our bodies at risk, emotional danger of being made to feel inferior or unworthy, financial danger of having no options and being at the mercy of a man, and on and on it goes.

Is it any wonder that the image of a heavenly female defender is so attractive? Don't we all sometimes want to hide behind the skirt of a larger-than-life mother who is able to always keep us safe, always know our needs, always stand ready to protect us from being wronged? A mother who can show up for us in ways that perhaps our human mothers couldn't—or wouldn't?

A societal foundation that makes women feel invalidated, inferior, and endangered is fertile ground for what author Bethany Webster calls "the mother wound." Kelly McDaniel's book title is *Mother Hunger*. These terms are sometimes used interchangeably, but for our purposes let's define the mother wound as the original pain inflicted by our childhood relationships with our mothers, and mother hunger as the ongoing result of that wound.

Some of us live our adult lives as motherless daughters, whether because our moms have died or because narcissism, addiction, or abuse has made them unavailable to us. In relationships like these, the mother wound is deep, obvious, and excruciatingly painful. On the other hand, some of us had early relationships with our mothers that met our emotional and psychological needs entirely; we enjoyed a secure attachment and appropriate protection, nurture, and guidance. For women like these, the prospect of a mother wound might not carry much personal resonance. But the truth is, most of us fall somewhere in the middle.

And while our personal relationships with our actual mothers (and *their* relationships with *theirs*) matter a great deal, they're not the end of the story. Even in the most extreme cases, the source of the mother wound is not entirely individual responsibility; it's also the toxic conditions we have long required women to exist in. Your mother could not give much more than what she herself was given—and the same is true of *her* mother, and the same is true of you as a mother, unless you do some serious inner work.

In Webster's paradigm, the mother wound is fourfold: personal, cultural, spiritual, and planetary. We all experience these on a spectrum, but even women who don't bear a personal mother wound must still reckon with the other three levels. Since this wound is specific to patriarchal societies, if you live in one it is practically unavoidable.

Why would it be specific to patriarchal societies? Glad you asked. Let's start by identifying some of the most fundamental principles of patriarchy as a system of social organization. The continuation of patriarchy depends on things like prioritizing men, suppressing feelings, normalizing violated boundaries, approving violence, shaming the expression of needs, and valuing production over rest. This list is not exhaustive, but it's a start.

In case you didn't notice, this is not a list that makes for a healthy human. Nor is it aligned with instincts that come naturally to females. And yet it is the basis for the society within which we must survive.

But we are not only expected to survive in it; we are expected to raise children within it—and sacrifice ourselves to whatever extent is needed to do so. Webster writes, "As a result of these limiting beliefs and superhuman standards, women forgo their dreams, bottle up their desires, and suppress their needs in favor of meeting the cultural ideal of what womanhood should be. This pressure is suffocating for women, engendering rage, depression, anxiety, and overall emotional pain, which . . . is then unconsciously passed on to daughters through subtle or even aggressive forms of emotional abandonment (mothers can't be emotionally present when stressed), manipulation (shame, guilt, and obligation), or rejection."

The child's immature brain then processes her mother's reaction by internalizing the belief that there is something wrong, not with the environment or even with her mother, but with *her*. This is the essence of the mother wound, and in the majority of our families it has been passed on from generation to generation.

As I write this, my maternal grandmother is nearing her ninetieth birthday. Nell is a kindhearted but no-nonsense woman, the sort of woman who will feed a stray dog for a decade but never let it step foot inside the house. After my grandfather passed away, six years ago, she sold their farm to my uncle but continued mowing the acre-long yard on her John Deere every week for as long as she could manage it. She is short and stout, with thick white hair and fluffy breasts that I would lay against like a pillow as a little girl.

My grandmother was eighteen years old when she stood before a little country church congregation and her father "gave her" in marriage to her husband. She was nineteen when she became a mother, and shortly after that her own mother died, leaving Nell to help raise her younger sisters while raising her own toddler daughter—my mom. My grandmother worked for decades in an office with no female managers or supervisors, eventually becoming the very first. At the beginning of her career, women could not have their own checking accounts or credit cards.

Mother hunger is "passed from grandmother to mother to daughter," McDaniel writes. "The belief that women are somehow less than men damages our bond with each other as we pass our internalized beliefs about our body, worth, and power to the next generation." The field of epigenetics tells us that our environment can actually change our genes—and the genes we pass on to our descendants. McDaniel emphasizes this means that toxic stress, sexual objectification, disempowerment, and suppressed needs experienced by the women in your family line really did affect your mother. Hence, they really do affect you.

I think about these little woundings in my family line. The *Who gives this woman?*, and the *Stop by Daddy's to cook for your sisters before going home to cook for your own family,* and the *Women simply aren't manager material,* and the *Your money belongs to your husband.*

These little woundings. These soul squashers. These messages pounded into my grandmother's bones. I wonder about how they affected her in ways she might still not know. I wonder about how they affected my mother, that little girl caught between two families, the one with a mother who must have been desperately grieving her own mother. And I wonder about how they affect me, these little woundings of the grandmother whom I love very much. I think about how all three of us carry these little woundings—and so many more that I will never know, but that still I bear—in our bodies.

We pass on more to one another than just height and nose shape and eye color. We pass on longing and loss and resiliency and trauma and grief and desire and fear and need. We pass on every way this world has enthralled us and every way this world has terrified us. We pass it all down; it all lives right here in our cells, making us hungry for we know not what.

And if we don't learn to befriend it, our hunger will eat us alive.

*   *   *

When Eric and I were in the process of adopting our first child, and through the years after he came home, we tried to get as much education as possible about attachment theory and the effects of the early trauma of being separated from one's biological mother. We found that the science is sobering: the basis of a person's lifelong psychobiological well-being is established between the time of conception and age two.

Notice the timetable is tracked from conception, not birth; for from the last trimester of pregnancy through age two, the brain doubles in size. During this period of rapid brain growth, infants cannot regulate their own emotions—they need their mothers, whom they perceive to be an extension of themselves, to translate feelings of love and safety. It's almost like mama and baby share a brain for nearly three years!

So what happens if that connection is severed through a mother's death, abandonment, illness, or lack of emotional availability? As you can imagine, any of these experiences has a tremendous effect on the child's development—even if loving and attentive caregivers swoop in immediately. The loss of what was meant to be, what had already begun in utero, still exists. And while a healthy, happy, thriving future is still available to the child given the right circumstances and support, the grief (conscious or unconscious) of what was lost will never completely disappear.

I knew this in the context of adoption, and the first time I read Thérèse of Liseux's account of her childhood, I was only a couple of years removed from my deep dive into attachment theory. But at the time, I missed Thérèse's glaring mother wound completely. I couldn't see it, despite reading that her mother was gravely ill during her pregnancy, had to entrust her baby's care to a wet nurse, and died when Thérèse was only four years old.

But she still had a doting father and a host of other supporting characters in her life, so the story struck me as sad but not particularly traumatic.

It wasn't until I revisited *Story of a Soul* a decade later, with more life experience and a year of my own therapy under my belt, that I was able to see the deep grief for what it was. Thérèse recounts how her entire personality changed after her mother's death, her happy disposition turning timid and "sensitive to an excessive degree." She cried at the drop of a hat and avoided interacting with anyone who was family. By her own account, she would struggle with depression for the rest of her childhood.

But even then, it wasn't Thérèse's stories of those formative early years that turned the lights on in my brain; it was the way she spoke again and again about the maternal care of her Mother Prioress at Carmel—who just so happened to be her older sister Pauline.

Pauline's nurturance of Thérèse didn't originate in the convent. On the day of their mother's funeral, four-year-old Thérèse turned to her big sister "as though the future had torn aside its veil," threw herself into Pauline's arms, and cried, "Well, as for me, it's Pauline who will be my Mama!" The older sibling, not even a teenager herself, took up the mantle tenderly.

The fact that the sister who helped raise Thérèse could be a superior in her convent and serve as a surrogate mother was an incredible grace. Mother Agnes (as Pauline was known) provided spiritual and emotional maternal support and cared physically for Thérèse through her battle with tuberculosis, ultimately staying at her deathbed to midwife her into the afterlife. This is a sacred relationship. But that doesn't take away the grief of the original mother wound that necessitated it.

Was the longing to heal her mother wound what attracted

Thérèse to the convent? Surely it wasn't the only reason; still, I can't help but think it played a part. A lifetime spent in the committed, unwavering presence of a group of women older than she? The fact that two of her older sisters—both mother figures to her in their own right—had taken the vows a few years before? Carmelite life fit Thérèse's needs like a glove.

Thérèse loved her father, but she needed a mother. And this lack unconsciously affected everything she did. Because for Thérèse, as for so many women today and throughout history, the mother wound was a relentless companion.

* * *

There once was a mother who wished for a child as white as snow, as red as blood, and as black as her embroidery frame. The earth heard the desire of the woman's heart and she gave birth to a daughter with white skin, red lips, and jet-black hair. And then, the woman died.

One year later the child's father remarried, taking for his bride a woman beautiful but riddled with envy. Each day she would stand before a magical looking glass and ask to see the fairest one in the kingdom—and each day, the looking glass would assure her that it was she. Until the day it could no longer.

When the girl with red lips and black hair was just seven years old, the looking glass reported that she was now the fairest in all the land. The stepmother went mad with jealous rage and employed a huntsman to take the girl into the forest and cut out her heart. But once the two were in the belly of the woods, the huntsman couldn't do it. He released the girl and carved out a wild boar's heart instead, bringing it to the stepmother, who ate it mercilessly with a knife and fork.

Meanwhile, the young girl was taken into the home of seven

dwarfs, where she was loved and honored. But the looking glass reported her, and three times the stepmother disguised herself and attempted the murder on her own. Three times she was thwarted.

Eventually, the girl grew to the age of marriage and captured the heart of a prince. When the stepmother got to the wedding and saw the bride she knew only too well, she was paralyzed by hatred. To punish her for her evil deeds, the happy newlyweds forced her to wear scalding hot iron shoes and dance until she fell down dead.

You surely recognize the story of Snow White, though the gruesomeness of the Brothers Grimm version may surprise you if you've been familiar with only the sanitized Disney interpretation.

This beloved fairy tale is a fascinating elaboration on the dangers of the mother wound that are felt but rarely articulated—right down to the jealousy a mother may feel over her daughter's youth and beauty (notably, things that give a woman value and power in a patriarchal society). Snow White's embodiment of what the stepmother was losing with age served as a brutal reminder to the queen that her time for influence, esteem, and security was coming to an end.

But it's not just age and physical attractiveness that can elicit a mother's unwanted feelings of envy. Many women find themselves unwittingly jealous of the lifestyles, career opportunities, reproductive choice, education, egalitarian marriages, inner healing, or other successes of their adult daughters. Under the cruel umbrella of patriarchy, advancements for modern women can trigger feelings of pain, injustice, and grief in members of the previous generation, who had fewer options and rights. And yet most of us are not conscious enough to make sense of those feelings. We are just trying to survive here.

That's why, over two hundred years after the tale was written, the story of Snow White still hits a nerve. That's why fairy tales are a true art form.

The mother wound's prominence in the story of Snow White is far from an isolated case: unconscious wrestling with the mother figure is one of the most consistent themes in the catalog of fairy tales. Think about it: *Cinderella, The Little Mermaid, Little Red Riding Hood, Hansel and Gretel*. Mothers in fairy tales are almost guaranteed to be either dead or absent. You'll be hard-pressed to find an exception. And in the void they leave, danger emerges—usually in the form of a wicked stepmother or a cunning witch.

This isn't a coincidence. Fairy tales are composed with the intent of giving shape to a child's unconscious. In *The Uses of Enchantment,* Bruno Bettelheim suggests that it feels safer for children to work out complicated feelings and urges about and against their mothers in a secondary way—with a buffer, if you will. Instead of naming faults or critiques of the most important figure in their life, children can wrestle through those things in the name of a stepmother or a witch.

As children, we are no fools: we know we need our mothers for survival. But we are also attuned to the cultural ideal of upholding the myth of the perfect mother at all costs. Children intuit that it is unwise to criticize the one person who is hailed for sacrificing herself for you; who is put on a social pedestal as ever gentle, kind, nurturing, and attentive; who is assumed to be an icon of maternal care.

We feel this as adults, too. Women who have painful relationships with their mothers are often shamed or labeled ungrateful for expressing them. As a culture, we are slow to make room for a maternal narrative that is anything but comfortable, for doing so would force questions about the cost of patriarchy and thereby threaten the very foundation of our society. So instead we silence those who try to tell the truth.

But back to the fairy tale. To my mind, there is another layer of wisdom in developing a children's story around the absence of a mother: it requires that the young girl be centered instead. It is up to her to survive, to find protection, to outwit the enemy. The story becomes hers. And while part of her would prefer to be shepherded by a nurturing and protective mother, another part of her is fascinated by the prospect of being the central woman in the narrative. She is curious about her own power.

This awakening is a big part of the process of nursing the mother wound. As women arrive at the place of recognizing and naming the wound, we may begin to trust our intuition, explore possibilities, and chart our own course.

But, fairy tales teach us, first we must let ourselves feel afraid. We will likely spend some time in a proverbial wilderness. We might die a metaphorical death. We will definitely grieve a loss.

In the beginning, embarking on the journey of self-mothering requires a lot of discomfort. Many of us will experience what McDaniel calls "disenfranchised grief," meaning a grief that cannot be openly acknowledged. Public grieving and collective grief rituals like funerals and memorials are part of how we are hardwired to cope with painful loss. Being unable to do that is a second loss compounded on the first.

McDaniel's recommendations for nursing the mother wound include allowing yourself time to wallow in previously suppressed feelings, finding belonging with a group of women, drawing any necessary boundaries with your mother, and getting a good therapist. But the recommendation for the healing process that I found most interesting was what she calls finding a "celestial mother," which apparently is what I was doing through my devotion to Mary without even realizing it.

Imaging God in the feminine can be a powerful practice, and we have already explored the precedent for doing so within Christianity. In addition to Julian of Norwich's Mother God, we have Lady Wisdom (Sophia) in the book of Proverbs or—going back to our roots—Shekinah in the Jewish tradition. But a celestial mother doesn't have to be God, per se. Any of the mystics in this book could serve you well, as could Mary. If you feel pain in relation to institutional church figures or symbols, you might find comfort in just the nurture of Mother Earth.

*   *   *

Did Thérèse of Lisieux live long enough to learn to re-mother the little girl inside who so deeply felt the wound of maternal loss? We can't know for sure, of course, but it doesn't seem like it. As her life came to an end while she was still in her early twenties, the sheltered nun presented herself very much as a daughter. It wouldn't be fair to expect more from such a young woman, yet I can't help but wonder what riches she would have taught us on this topic had she lived to old age—especially considering that many of the mystics we have studied didn't come into their own until after age forty.

Although her journey of healing was cut short, it made an indelible mark on Thérèse's spiritual life. The "little way" of Thérèse of Lisieux was birthed out of a primal need to have her inner child nurtured by—you guessed it—a cosmic mother. Unlike Julian of Norwich, Thérèse never addressed Jesus in such terms, but her way of relating to the divine very much falls within the paradigm.

A quick scan of her writings reveals the following phrases, each used countless times in reference to herself: *childish desires, only a child, weak and little, my littleness, powerless and weak, childish simplicity, little flower, little bird, weak one, my childishness.* This is far from an exhaustive list. It would be fascinating to find out exactly how many times Thérèse refers to herself in infantilized language. (But not fascinating enough to actually be the one to do the counting, so I'll pass.)

So marked was she by the need for perpetual childishness that the official name she took upon her entrance to the Carmelite convent was Thérèse of the Child Jesus. In her writings, she once challenged Jesus to find a soul "weaker and littler" than hers, certain that to do so would be impossible.

While such descriptors might feel disempowering and self-deprecating to us, they had the opposite effect on Thérèse. So ravenous was her mother hunger that the most empowering thing she could imagine was being nurtured, protected, and held.

Would Thérèse's needs and spirituality have evolved had she lived longer? Probably. But as a young woman with a mother wound the size of France, she craved the permission to crawl up onto the lap of God (aka a cosmic mother) for guidance and care as a little child. She needed to be free to stay small, to not grow up motherless, to comfort that four-year-old girl inside who desperately needed to feel her mama's touch.

She needed to be re-mothered; and she knew just the One who could do it.

"I read these words coming from the mouth of Eternal Wisdom: *'Whoever is a LITTLE ONE, let them come to me.'* . . . I continued my search and this is what I discovered: *'As one whom a mother caresses, so will I comfort you; you shall be carried at the breasts, and upon the knees they shall caress you.'* Ah! Never did words more tender and more melodious come to give joy to my soul. . . . And for this I had no need to grow up, but rather I had to remain little and become this more and more."

Questions for Prayer and Reflection

1. Spend some time contemplating the possibility of all four layers of the mother wound (personal, cultural, spiritual, planetary) in your life. Do any stand out with particular resonance?
2. Have you ever had a conversation about this topic with another woman or women? If not, what might it feel like to share your experience openly?
3. What feelings arise when you consider the idea of finding a cosmic mother to help you on your healing journey? Does that feel comforting or frightening? What would some comfortable initial steps toward this idea look like for you?

CATHERINE OF SIENA

CHAPTER ELEVEN

Balancing Action and Contemplation

When I was a college senior I sat across from my mom at a folksy, locally owned breakfast café in the Texas town where I'd grown up and explained why it was imperative that I move to Missouri after graduation to be part of the 24/7 prayer movement at the International House of Prayer. Yes, that's correct: I had informed my mother that after completing years of fancy private university education I was going to move states away to sit in a room with a bunch of strangers and pray all day at a place called IHOP.

Needless to say, she wasn't thrilled.

Up to this point I had always been a person of action, raised by two people committed to action. As a young teen I had volunteered at an animal shelter. In high school I had visited a local nursing home once a week. As a college student I had jumped full throttle into my church's tutoring program for at-risk kids. Once I even cold-called a zoo to offer my help. I'd always had an insatiable hunger to make a difference in the world, a sense of moral duty to the people (and animals) I share the earth with. Signing myself up for a modern-day cloister didn't sound much like me. My mom moved her pancake around with her fork, thinking.

"Well, Shan, I know you've really been growing spiritually

these past couple of years, and that makes me so happy," she allowed. I waited for the *but,* and it came. "But I have to say, I'm a little skeptical of a group that closes themselves off from the world to pray. It doesn't sound much like what Jesus did. Jesus was always with the people—helping people."

In my youthful—okay, egotistical—naïveté, I explained to my mom why round-the-clock prayer was such important work. Probably something about Mary and Martha and *sitting at the feet of Jesus.* We found some middle ground and, she having said her piece and I having said mine, eventually moved on. But her discomfort pricked at something inside me—probably because it sounded too much like my own conscience.

I did end up spending a year at that IHOP (sadly, very few waffles were had) before moving on. Teaching ballet to low-income kids in Indonesia, becoming an adoptive parent, joining a Catholic Worker community in Texas, and eventually working as an editor for a progressive newspaper—these have all felt more aligned with who I am and what I value. Nearly twenty years after my time in the prayer movement, I don't regret it as such, but it is certainly light-years away from how I currently understand the divine and live my spirituality. The short version? Mama was right.

But the pendulum is always swinging, and it can be just as dangerous when it goes too far out on one side as when it swings too far on the other. And it seems like in the last decade, for me and for many whose circles intersect with mine, there has been a lot of call to action without a nourished, sustainable inner life. Ever since the volatile 2016 presidential race and election, followed by the #MeToo movement, the Covid pandemic, and the racial reckoning of 2020, there has been no end to awareness to be raised, injustice to be corrected, and wrongdoing to be called out. There is always a new petition to be signed, another group to be joined, another action to be taken; always more to do to "be the change." Activism burnout is real. Compassion fatigue is common. We simply aren't wired to hold so much injustice for such an extended time with no break. We must have spiritual fuel to bolster us with hope and love. As the saying goes, we can't pour from an empty cup.

But the solution isn't to turn our backs on the needs of the world. We're not ostriches here; our heads do not belong in the sand. We should not feel forced to choose between taking care of ourselves and taking care of those with whom we share this earth. There must be an integration of the two. There has to be a third way.

Catherine Benincasa was born in Siena, Italy, on March 25, 1347, and experienced immediate loss: the twin with whom she had shared a womb died upon their birth. The Benincasa family were no strangers to death: the twins were the twenty-third and twenty-fourth children birthed by their mother, with only half surviving into adolescence. And when Catherine was just a year old, the bubonic plague hit Siena, the first of two outbreaks she would live through in her hometown. But the most devastating loss in her early life was the death of her beloved older sister, who died while giving birth when Catherine was just coming of age.

Such a tumultuous backdrop feels like an apt introduction to a mystic who once said, "My nature is fire." She wasn't wrong. Catherine of Siena was passionate, determined, opinionated, and, dare I say, a bit of a drama queen. She experienced her first vision of Jesus and the apostles at age six and soon after made a secret vow of celibacy, too young to even understand sex but knowing she would never consent to belonging to anyone but God.

When she heard about Saint Euphrosyne, who disguised herself as a boy and ran away from home to join a monastery and live for four decades as a male, Catherine dreamed of following suit. But the closest she came was sneaking out of the house to the nearby Vallepiatta to experiment with living as a hermit in a grotto in the limestone hills. There she did indeed have a mystical experience, falling into a trance for several hours. But when she came to, she felt God reveal to her that she was not meant to be a hermit, so she innocently returned home to an unsuspecting family.

Catherine was only thirteen years old when her parents and older brothers began making marriage plans on her behalf, but she adamantly fought against them, much to their distress. They went back and forth over who had the final say, until the day Catherine left the house and returned home having sheared the hair off her own head. Suffice it to say, the family *lost their shit*. "You wicked girl," said her mother, "do you imagine that you can escape our authority by cutting your hair? It will grow again, and you shall be married, even if it breaks your heart. You shall never have any peace or quiet until you give in and do as we say."

Lapa Benincasa wasn't bluffing. The family did their best to make Catherine's life miserable. She lost the right to her own room and had to share with a brother; they fired the housemaid and made Catherine do all the washing, cooking, and serving; they teased and scolded her incessantly. But in the midst of it all, Catherine learned to find communion with the Spirit inside her; she found an inner monastic cell where she could be alone with her Beloved.

When Catherine finally felt she had the fortitude to tell her parents about the vow of chastity she had taken years before, she did so with such firm resolution that they knew there was no use arguing with her. They gave her a three-by-nine-foot cell in the house to use as her own room and released her from all duties besides her commitment to prayer.

This was progress, but it wasn't enough to satisfy Catherine. She was still young and unsure of exactly how this calling within her would unfold, but she knew it was more than just praying as an isolated individual. She wanted to be part of something bigger.

There was a Third Order Dominican group in Siena known as the Mantellate, and Catherine took notice of them. They were laypeople, not nuns, but had taken vows to live out the spirituality of Saint Dominic in public life, mostly through works of mercy. Many were widows. All were advanced in years. When Catherine expressed her desire to join them, they looked on her with uncertainty. It took her mother Lapa's most persuasive tactics to convince the Mantellate to accept her teenage daughter; but luckily, the apple didn't fall far from the tree. Lapa was as stubborn as her daughter, and, eventually, she wore the old women down.

Most people—even most Catholics—assume that the esteemed Saint Catherine of Siena, doctor of the Church and one of the best known of the Christian mystics, was a nun. But this is a misconception we can fairly blame on the fact that she, like the other Mantellates of Siena, chose to wear a habit. Seeing her represented in art and icons presents an understandable point of confusion to our modern senses.

But no, she never lived in a convent—first she kept her cell at her parents' house and later lived with various female friends— and she never answered to a Mother Superior. She made her own rules and her own decisions. Catherine of Siena was a laywoman through and through, which makes the fact that her advice would later be sought after by princes and popes all the more remarkable.

In 1364, at the age of nineteen, Catherine of Siena took the vows of a Third Order Dominican. But in classic Catherine style, she did it her own way. Instead of jumping headlong into the group's many acts of service and renowned public ministry, Catherine spent three years in total seclusion, leaving her cell in her parents' home only to attend Mass and speaking only to her confessor.

Was she discerning a calling of contemplation versus action? Had she set this period of time as preparation before entering public ministry? Did she have a plan at all? We don't know. But we do know that she decided not to stay in that cell forever. After three years, she describes having a vision of Jesus calling her to leave her self-imposed cloister, step out into the world, and be a woman of the people.

*   *   *

In the Ignatian spiritual tradition that has so profoundly shaped my way of being, one of the foundational values is to strive to be "a contemplative in action." I like the way spiritual director and Ignatian teacher Becky Eldredge explains it:

"A contemplative in action means being a woman and man of prayer who lives out in the world. . . . There is an interior life that seeks to grow deeper and deeper in a relationship with God and to still oneself in order to better hear God's voice within us. . . . What transpires in our contemplative life of prayer calls us outward into the world."

Most of us experience one of these—either action or contemplation—as coming more naturally than the other, depending on factors like personality, mental health, family culture, theology, employment, social circles, and the like. Sometimes our inclination changes according to our stage of life. But whether we tend to be more active or more contemplative, most of us will have to put greater intentionality toward the practice of one than the other in order to keep a harmonious balance between the two. Because things can get out of whack really fast.

Those who are drawn to contemplation are engaging in dynamic and important work, and that should never be minimized. And, contrary to what it may seem, contemplation is not an individualistic path. When done well, it is often the way of healing generational trauma within a family, providing spiritual guidance for a group, offering observations to the public through the arts, and more. But the gift must be used mindfully, so that contemplation doesn't become an excuse to turn inward and disengage from the rest of society.

On the other hand, we have all met or heard from activists who lack a true spiritual rootedness. (If you haven't, then just dip your toes into the waters of social media for about half a second.) They might speak the truth, but their tone, language, and delivery are so callous that it doesn't matter. No minds are being changed; no hearts are being won over. They are so tired and angry that they're actually repelling anyone who might otherwise be drawn to their message. If the whole point of their work is to convince people that empathy matters, their approach is not very effective.

Likewise, we all know someone who is in a helping profession and whose mental, emotional, spiritual, and even physical health is fried—maybe that someone is you. They are doing vital work as social workers, teachers, therapists, doctors, nurses, et cetera, but they have expended every ounce of themselves in the process. Hanging on for dear life, they are burned out and ready to quit. They know their work matters, but the collateral damage to their souls is just not sustainable.

I have to believe that we can keep on giving a damn *and* tend to the roots of our souls. We can and we must. Because for us to do the work well, to be in it for the long haul, our action must come from wholeness and not from wounds.

Women of color have been teaching us about the need for contemplation to balance action for a long time. We are lucky to be living in a time when many women of color are publicly providing leadership in this area in clear, organized ways.

Tricia Hersey is the founder of the Nap Ministry, whose motto is "Rest is Resistance." The Nap Ministry was founded in 2016 and uses performance art, site-specific installations, and community organizing to install sacred and safe spaces for communities to rest together as a tool for radical healing.

Dr. Christena Cleveland is the founder of the Center for Justice and Renewal, which serves to help Black activists' "understanding of the social realities that maintain injustice while also stimulating the soul's enormous capacity to resist and transform those realities."

Dr. Barbara Holmes is on faculty at the Center for Action and Contemplation in Albuquerque. As a scholar of African American spirituality, she teaches on the divine imagination and wisdom in times of crisis.

Kaitlin Curtice is a Potawatomi author and speaker whose work encompasses both advocacy for Indigenous justice and the rhythms of earth-based spiritual care required to sustain such advocacy.

These women—and many more like them—are the prophets of our modern age. They expose the lies of white supremacist patriarchy, which try to convince us that rest is dangerous, production rules, connection to the divine is unnecessary, and self-care is for the weak. Women of color have always pointed us toward a better way, a way that refuses to sacrifice wholeness as a means to an end, a way that nurtures and nourishes the entire human person.

*   *   *

It's a shame that Catherine of Siena didn't have such wise women to mother her through her own ministry, for their gentle guidance might have added many years to her life. Then again, it might not have mattered—for once Catherine set her mind on something, it was impossible to change.

This was the case when she began her public ministry and life of service as a Mantellate: when Catherine of Siena finally jumped, it was right into the deep end.

Nearly overnight, Catherine's life became a constant stream of tending to the needs of others, moving from the prisons to the hospitals to the streets without a break. On any given day she was an advocate for the imprisoned, a nurse for the diseased, a peacemaker for broken families, or a mediator for the hierarchy of the Roman Catholic Church. While Catherine had her fair share of haters, most people took appreciative note of her devotion to them. Her nickname around town was Beata Popolana, or "the blessed child of the people." Biographer Sigrid Undset notes that she seemed to have never been alone. This is not hyperbole; this is fact.

It goes without saying that to live such a life is admirable and deeply loving. In her famous work *Dialogue,* Catherine relates being told by God, "Your service is of no use to Me, it is by serving your neighbor that you can serve Me." She took that mandate seriously.

Catherine wanted nothing more than to alleviate the suffering of her fellow humans in the name of the God she knew. But in order to do so, she repressed each and every need she had until she was reduced to nothing. She insisted on being in a constant state of physical denial. Not only did she not rest but she almost never slept. She practiced self-flagellation, at least in her younger years. Her fasting was so extreme that she eventually lost the ability to swallow and digest her food. Tragically, Catherine died without finding the compassion for herself that she had in such surplus for others.

Catherine was scrupulous and hard on herself, so much so that reading her words can make your heart ache. For example, she believed her inability to chew, swallow, and digest food was punishment for the sin of gluttony because she had been "so greedy for fruit" as a little child. Even in the context of the theology of the Middle Ages, this is a red flag of a woman unwell.

While I have no professional credentials to make this claim, as I am neither a historian nor a psychologist, I believe there is ample reason to think that Catherine suffered from anorexia. Her disordered relationship with food far surpassed the bounds of spiritual practice, and her history of self-harm and extreme perfectionism align with the nonfood elements of the eating disorder as well. Most telling is the physiological damage that resulted from years of "fasting," which contributed to, if not entirely caused, her early death.

I'll be honest: when I started my research on Catherine of Siena, I was expectantly looking for answers on how to balance a life of justice and mercy with soul care and restorative prayer. Knowing that she was a woman of fervent action and also a mystic, I assumed Catherine would be the perfect guide for this important chapter. As it turns out, she is—but for reasons quite the opposite from my initial thinking. Catherine is the right mystic to teach us about balancing action and contemplation not because she perfected it but because she was so horribly, terribly, unequivocally bad at it. Which, I think, makes for a much more interesting story.

No matter what her intentions were when she betrothed herself to Christ, or professed vows as a Mantellate, Catherine's reality was that she never did find a way to balance action and contemplation. It seemed to be either/or for her. Her driven and scrupulous nature resisted the more healthy push and pull that her beloved Jesus had modeled in his own ministry. Catherine was either praying in a locked room for years or working herself to the bone. Her mind could never get the swinging pendulum to find the middle.

So her body and soul had to do it for her.

One of the hallmarks of Catherine of Siena's life was her frequent—sometimes daily—ecstasies, in which she would have clear dialogue with God and visions that caused her to lose track of time and break from reality. In the beginning these happened during periods of intense prayer, but later they began to come upon her even in public: after every time she consumed the Eucharist at Mass, for instance, and when seated in regular old conversation with people around a kitchen table.

It goes without saying that ecstasies such as these are spiritually profound and endlessly fascinating. But I'm a bit more interested in the human side of them. Might these frequent trances have been a solution for the extreme deprivation of her body and soul's need for sustenance, sleep, stress relief, and rest? Might these episodes have been brief respites demanded by her physicality to relieve the burden on her exhausted human limits?

Contemporary author Murray Bodo, OFM, says legitimate spiritual ecstasies can be judged by whether they rejuvenate the mystic for a life of service. He writes, "The true mystic afterward returns to an intense gospel life of service to others, especially the sick and those on the margins of society . . . the ecstasy or vision does not drive the mystic inward to self-centeredness, but takes her out of herself into God, only to return recharged."

The human consciousness, and the human body, can only take so much. I can't help wondering if these ecstasies—which she could not prevent, predict, or control—were actually protecting Catherine from fatal brokenness and burnout. Sure, they also earned her the scorn of plenty of people, some of her fellow Mantellates included; what would have happened, though, if she hadn't had the grace of such mental and emotional reprieves?

But even ecstasies and trances couldn't hold off the inevitable forever. Catherine Benincasa died young, at just thirty-three years old, after having been deteriorating for years from pushing herself to extremes. At the end of her life she was so emaciated that her mother later commented to a biographer that she looked like a shadow. (Her mother, by the way, lived to be eighty-nine years old, so one wonders what long life Catherine might herself have had if things had been different.) She could no longer swallow any food except the Eucharist.

In her lifetime, Catherine made an incredible impact. In addition to tending suffering people with tenderness and care, she helped reform the Catholic Church at a critical time and on a massive scale. But tending the wounds of a dying leper was, to Catherine, of equal value to writing letters to admonish powerful cardinals. Attending the execution of a prisoner she had been praying with was no less important than traveling to France to convince the pope to return to Rome (which he ultimately did, on her advice).

Catherine of Siena's story is equal parts inspiring and sobering, an example of the formidable power of what a woman can do, and a warning of what happens when we put everyone ahead of ourselves as we are doing it. Her voice calls to us from across the centuries, a siren of caution sounding for women to *care,* yes, but to *take care,* too.

May we listen and learn.

Questions for Prayer and Reflection

1. Which comes more naturally to you, contemplation or action? Do you try to intentionally work the muscle of the one that does not come naturally? Have you found ways to do so that feel true to who you are?

2. Has there been a period in your life, however long or brief, that you felt contemplation and action were held in healthy balance? What do you observe about that time?

3. Our bodies tend to let us know when we are doing too much action and not enough contemplation, or rest. What signs has your body given you to slow down and seek rejuvenation?

CHAPTER TWELVE

Horror, Gore, Death,
and the Necessity of Facing Our Shadows

Between writing the previous chapter and this one, I almost died.

Have you ever nearly died with one chapter left to go in a book? I don't recommend it. Not only because it throws your print time line completely off schedule, but because everything in the "before" feels disconnected from—nearly irrelevant to—things in the "after." Remind me again what I wrote in the first eleven chapters. Because it was a lifetime ago.

I will say this: be careful what you ask a saint for. Months ago, I thought long and hard about what the theme of this chapter should be, based on the life and writings of Catherine of Siena. The topic of women in church leadership is low-hanging fruit, but my intuition told me that wasn't it. What I found myself most curious about was the absolute goriness of Catherine's life, the way she seemed to be constantly surrounded by wounds, sickness, grotesque visions, dismembered body parts (we'll get to it), and death. I wanted to write about *that*—but from what angle? And what did I know about horror?

Now I'm not saying Catherine of Siena put an infection in my body and gave me septic shock. But I'm also not saying she didn't. One thing I do know is that she was with me for eight days in the hospital, gently nudging this chapter along in the direction she wanted it to go. Through blood transfusions and IVs, she flowed into my veins. During CT scans and MRIs, she entered liminal spaces with me. While I slept through an appendectomy and through days of strong narcotics, she guided my unconscious state. When they pulled tubes out of my neck and stomach, she was in my thoughts.

I have no doubt in my mind that there are people more qualified than I am to write this chapter. But I was the one with the desire and availability, so I kind of imagine Catherine sighing, shrugging, and being like, "Okay, let's go. I can work with this." I am an expert on nothing—least of all death—but, as always, I have thoughts, curiosities, and questions. May it be enough. Let's begin.

*   *   *

There are dozens of good reasons not to align oneself with a particular religious tradition. Most religions have done quite a bit of damage to humankind, after all, and I understand that trauma makes it impossible for some to stay in a religion and also be healthy at the end of the day. I will cast my vote for mental, emotional, and spiritual health every single time.

And yet I do believe there are specific gifts that tried-and-true religious traditions can offer humanity, gifts that have value for the soul but that we are not likely to access without a bit of nudging. The intentional examination of our wrongdoing ("sin") is one. The acknowledged inevitability of death—and the question of what to do with that fact—is another.

But my favorite of these gifts as a Christian has been the inescapable meditation on materiality, or what we call "incarnational thinking." A human woman giving birth to God. God becoming human. "The Word" becoming flesh. The Divine in bread, in wine, in a mustard seed. Christians across the aisle from one another can argue the core tenets of our theology all day long (and they do), but one thing about this religious tradition that demands our begrudging agreement is its adamant refusal to allow us to dissociate from our humanity.

Catholicism takes it up a notch. Here we name, image, and glorify martyrs; the more grotesque their stories, the more beloved they are likely to be. Saint Lawrence was burned alive in the year A.D. 258 for presenting before the emperor an assembly of people in poverty and daring to call them the Church's treasures. As he was publicly burned for his offense, Lawrence joked with his executioners that he was "done" on one side and should be flipped. He's now the patron saint of tanners and firefighters.

But stories aren't enough, for Catholics are a sensory people. We collect the relics of departed saints—body parts, bits of clothing, a handkerchief once sneezed into—and put them on display in our fanciest churches. Often they go on tour, bizarre circuses attracting new admirers from town to town. It is as odd a tradition as anything I could make up, but it's not without value: the physicality of such a scene tethers us to reality. *This is a body, this could be your body, and it matters that it was here.* The material is critical to the spiritual. We cannot have the latter without the former.

It's not just our relics that testify to this necessity. Church history—whether factual or fictionalized—teems with the fleshy physicality of what it means to have an incarnational faith. Christina the Astonishing came back from the dead during her funeral Mass, flew up to the rafters, and eventually had to go live in the trees with the birds because the smell of sin on humans was too rancid for her to bear. Catherine of Siena and Francis of Assisi famously bore the stigmata, the physical markings of Christ crucified on their hands, feet, head, or sides. And while we're back on the topic of Catherine, in one of her most celebrated visions, she received a wedding ring made of Jesus' foreskin. *The Defiant Middle* author Kaya Oakes notes that it wasn't rare for a medieval saint—female or male—to have visions of mystical weddings to Christ that involved wedding bands. "But only Catherine got a foreskin ring," Oakes quips. "She was that kind of special."

Catherine was indeed special, for better or worse. Few of our religious figures lived in such consistent proximity to gore, and not just because she devoted much of her time to the care of those who were ill. Catherine was determined to live fully present to the human condition; perhaps her commitment ran to a fault, as we examined in the last chapter, but it was remarkable nonetheless. This was a woman who refused to look away: from need, from horror, from God, from herself.

One of the clearest examples of this is the story of Catherine accompanying a young prisoner on his execution day. (History believes this to be Niccolò di Toldo, who was beheaded in Siena in 1375.) She visited him in prison, then took him to a priest who could offer the sacraments of confession and Eucharist. But at his death there was no priest beside him; there was only Catherine, who stepped onto the scaffold to offer a final blessing and gently cradle his head in her hands. When the executioner's blade came down upon his neck, it was Catherine who held his freshly slaughtered head.

Did she weep? Did she vomit? Did she scream? We'll never know. But she stayed. She held. She refused to look away. Good God, what a woman.

Little did she know that her own head would one day be separated from her body.

A few years after her death, it was decided that Catherine's remains should be moved from the outside to the inside of the church of Santa Maria sopra Minerva. It is now thought that it was this transfer that caused her head to be separated from her body, according to biographer Sigrid Undset, but other, more elaborate tales have been woven. The truth surrounding the circumstances of Catherine's wayward head may be lost to history, but that doesn't negate the fact that it can still be visited today, just waiting to greet you anytime you make it to Italy. The mystic's noggin was preserved in a gilded bronze bust and is still on display at the Saint Dominic Basilica in Siena, right next to one of her thumbs.

Author Kyle Smith calls Christianity a "cult of the dead," and you've gotta admit, he's not wrong. I mean, the whole gig revolves around a crucifixion; grappling with death is a necessarily looming part of the story. "Historically speaking," Smith writes, "it's not the sun-wrinkled smile on Mother Teresa that is the icon of Christian holiness—it's the char-grilled one on Lawrence." Or, I would submit, the skeletal one on the dismembered head of Catherine.

Is it any wonder that there is an entire canon of Catholic-themed movies in the horror film genre? The search for immortality is palpable, physical, here. We hope the structures and rituals offered can midwife us through the terrors that lurk under the surface of our souls. Grief. Fear. Death. So much of our reaching for religion is a reaching for the courage to ask questions about things too terrifying to touch alone.

*   *   *

A few years ago a Netflix horror series called *Midnight Mass* made a small but not insignificant splash in the online Catholic landscape. The premise piqued my interest: a small Catholic town in decline welcomes a young, new priest and experiences mysteries both glorious and ominous. Now look, I more or less kissed horror movies goodbye after my teen years, but the intrigue of a legitimate spirituality angle swayed me and I convinced Eric that we should give it a try.

We made it through all of three episodes.

The first episode started out harmless enough, with some good old-fashioned suspense techniques and a nuanced take on organized religion. The second episode got scary, but I could handle it. The third episode included someone hungrily drinking blood from an injured head, and that about sealed the deal for me. Clearly I was not the same girl who had once watched *I Know What You Did Last Summer* thirteen times. And don't even get me started on my Highly Sensitive Person spouse, who got up from the couch and frantically started watering plants in an unconscious effort to ward off the death spirits and keep life afloat.

We are a tender people in this house, is my point.

Apparently the last four episodes of the miniseries were incrementally more gruesome, but I'll never know. I worked hard to extract that charming little scene from my memory but, much to my chagrin, it came right back to me when I read Catherine of Siena's account of a vision she had of the crucified Christ drawing her mouth to his pierced side wound and inviting her to drink its blood. And, oh yes, she accepted the generous offer. Yes she did. It was *Midnight Mass* all over again up in my brain. *What is with this girl?* I wondered. *Every time I start to like her, she pulls out something batshit crazy!*

I did not love the grotesqueness of Catherine's life and imagination—I still don't. I'm not likely to ever be one of those people who watch horror movies for fun and have interesting philosophical conversations about them. (Part of me wants to be that kind of person, but not enough to actually, uh, do it.) Still, there is no denying that horror has a place in the spiritual life. Horror—whether that means relics, tales of burnt martyrs, or Halloween movies—asks us to look at the fears we're more inclined to ignore.

I remember being a teenager and confessing to my mom that I had a hunch I wouldn't live past my midtwenties. (I know, every mother's dream conversation with her child.) When I was in my early twenties—surprised, I suppose, to have made it to such a wizened old age—I became inwardly certain that I would one day be martyred. Fortunately, I had the good sense not to announce this to everyone I knew, but I did tell a few close friends whose religious fervor matched my own, and Eric was given a heads-up before we got engaged. I figured it was only fair to let him know he would probably be a widower.

But over time I aged and my brain wrapped up the last of its development, and, well, dying became less and less interesting. As it turned out, living was rather exciting too. So for the next fifteen years or so I barely gave my own death a passing thought—a luxury, I know. While Eric explored meditation techniques to face his own death anxiety, and while close friends fought off panic attacks on airplanes over the same, I just sort of . . . lived. With no strong feelings about my own future death one way or the other.

This, of course, was the "before times."

*   *   *

Sepsis happens when the body works so hard to fight an infection that it can no longer distinguish the enemy from itself: it poisons its own blood. In the worst cases, organs shut down, blood pressure plummets, and the heart weakens, sending the body into septic shock. In a misguided attempt to protect you, your own body tries to kill you. Correction: in a misguided attempt to protect me, my own body tried to kill me.

Do I feel grateful or do I feel terrified?

Yes. I do.

In her book *How We Live Is How We Die,* acclaimed thought leader and Buddhist nun Pema Chödrön outlines the physical sensations that accompany the five "stages of dissolution" experienced when a person nears death; they are the feeling of heaviness and being weighed down, unquenchable thirst, chills that cannot be warmed, abnormal breathing patterns, and, finally, the loss of breath entirely.

By the time I had been admitted into the ICU to receive blood pressure medicine, oxygen, and a blood transfusion, I had three of those five symptoms. I was suffering from a condition that could kill a person in twelve hours, and I'd likely had it for forty-eight. I didn't know the first thing about septic shock, but I did know that ICU nurses are famously hard to shake—and they were looking at me like they'd seen a ghost. Like they'd seen the shadow of death fall over a thirty-nine-year-old woman.

It was in the ICU that I first recognized the presence of death's possibility in my body. There, I touched a new kind of fear and grief and loss, without using those terms at all. No one on my medical team uttered the word *death* around me until days later, when I was in the clear and recovering on the general surgical floor. The mortality rate of septic shock is between 40 and 50 percent, I learned while trying to swallow Jell-O and stand on legs that felt about as firm.

The word *death* hadn't offered itself to me for use; not because I hadn't felt its nearness, but because putting language to it would have felt insufficient. As anemic as the blood in my veins. But even without invoking the word, I had known I was lingering in an in-between space; I recognized that the plane I was existing on was not one I had ever visited before. Like Catherine of Siena, I did not choose existential terror; it chose me.

I know that when I say things like *existential terror,* I can tend to freak people out. And, okay, *fair*. But I should clarify that I don't mean being consumed by a panicked sense of fear and anxiety. (Though I did experience those things after coming home from the hospital and having to figure out how to re-engage with "life as normal" after such a trauma.) No, I would argue that the kind of terror of which I speak is healthy—at least for a while. There is something appropriate about responding to a thing as enormous as the inevitability of your own death with intense awe, gripping fear, and holy trepidation. If we go through all of life having never felt that terror, even in glimpses, it's because we have never dared to hold death's gaze. And for creatures who are destined to perish, that is no kind of wisdom.

"Don't be afraid of your own shadow," Catherine of Siena reminds us. Colloquially, we have come to use this statement to mean the equivalent of "don't be a scaredy cat." But that is far from her original intent. In much of her writing, Catherine exhorts us to be willing to look at the shadow within that scares us or makes us uncomfortable, the parts of ourselves we don't want anyone to see, the parts of ourselves *we* don't want to see. The parts we can't control, the parts we can't reason with, the parts that don't comply, the parts we hate, the parts that terrify us with their enormity.

But to be afraid of one's shadow is to be afraid of oneself,

Catherine reminds us. For darkness, too, is instructive; darkness, too, has its place. Darkness, too, is its own form of light, if what we mean by light is a trustworthy guide.

Horror and gore offer us the rare invitation to face our own shadow, to learn not to fear it. They remind us that we are going to die—yes, you, you are going to die—and, unlike our religions, horror and gore don't let us do any spiritual bypassing around that fact. They don't wrap it up with a neat and tidy bow. They don't skip to the good part. They just let us be scared.

In Catherine of Siena's world, suffering waited at nearly every turn. Her hometown was ravaged by a plague that racked up the corpses of one-third of its inhabitants. Her beloved sister died in childbirth. Eight of her nieces and nephews died as children. Her ministry centered the terminally ill. Is it any wonder that Catherine had a morbid spiritual imagination? She needed that. It was the only way she could integrate the intensity of death's proximity with the demands of her everyday life. Folks needed prayer, needed comfort. There wasn't time to think about her PTSD, and, besides, everyone she knew lived with their own.

*   *   *

There was an old woman in Catherine's order named Andrea, who had breast cancer so advanced that half her chest became one large open wound, poisonous and rancid. The sight and smell were so horrific that almost no one would visit the woman; no one, of course, except Catherine.

Catherine committed to nursing the old woman until her death, coming to her home every day to feed Andrea, change the bandage, apply salve to the wound, and take care of other needs Andrea had, likely including toileting assistance. Andrea began commending Catherine to others as an angel and a saint, but Catherine knew the truth: she was revolted by Andrea's condition and never felt less holy than while warding off the horrific thoughts she had during her hours of care for the woman's decaying body. One day, she'd had enough of her own fear and hypocrisy: she picked up the bowl of water she'd been using to clean the wound, now full of pus and infection, and swallowed every last drop.

This story alone is enough to seal Catherine's position among the most memorable in the litany of Christian saints, but it also makes it a little too easy to write her off as mentally ill or dangerously scrupulous. I'm not sure Catherine was either of those things exactly. I think the truth is more complex than such reductions—and endlessly more interesting.

Horror and gore don't just demand we hold death's gaze; they also demand we behold that which terrifies and revolts us in our humanity, and this story from Catherine's life is a clear illustration of that fact. The story is often told as an example of her extreme commitment to fasting and penance. But that's not what Catherine describes. She tells us that before swallowing the unthinkable contents of the bowl, she readied herself with these words: "By the Life of the Almighty, by the beloved Bridegroom of my soul, you shall receive in your stomach what you feel such fear of."

Catherine didn't drink pus water in order to punish herself. She drank it to free herself from fear.

Do I believe God asked Catherine to drink the pus from a dying person's wounds? No, I don't. I don't believe God is into that kind of sadism. But the point isn't what I believe. The point is that *Catherine believed there was freedom for her in that action*. She believed that facing her deepest fear, her most intense revulsion, would free her inner self into deeper union with the Divine and with her fellow humans. We can judge her decision all day long, but the fact remains that it worked. She told her confessor that after that moment she never again experienced repulsion in Andrea's presence.

I can report that I myself drank no pus while in the hospital, and if that means I will never be as inwardly free as Catherine of Siena, I still have no regrets. I apologize if my lack of holiness disappoints you. However, on my third day in the ICU something happened that made a similar imprint on me.

It was determined that I needed to have an MRI of my digestive system. The appendectomy had been successful, but when the surgeons cut me open they discovered that my appendix was really only moderately inflamed. It merited removal, yes, but was not enough to trigger such a severe sepsis response, and the signs of Crohn's disease the GI doctor had so confidently predicted would be found in my intestines were all but absent when they took a look inside. And so I entered what would be a month of rigorous testing, starting with this MRI.

On this day I was still in excruciating pain, heavily medicated, and weaker than I'd been in all my life, including childbirth. Being transferred to and from the MRI took several hours—I was that slow—but it had to be done. At this point my spirit/soul/unconscious/what-have-you was still going bananas on me, and, every time I closed my eyes to rest or fall asleep, I was inundated with an onslaught of images, videos, voices, and thoughts. Perhaps biblical prophets would have called them "visions." They were more rapid-fire than I can explain, like someone shuffling cards containing everything in my brain, over and over and over again, as it tried to make sense of the trauma. The effect was

sometimes beautiful, sometimes interesting, sometimes annoy-
ing, and always overwhelming.

So when it happened again there on the MRI table, with the
loud whooshing sound of mechanical magic thrumming against
my ears, I gave way to its familiar visitation and watched as a
passive observer. But what came then was not the sort of thing
that had come before—or would again after. These were not
the glimpses I had grown accustomed to: not my boys laughing,
not my daughter reaching for me, not my father-in-law saying,
We have to trust God, in his simple, steadfast way; these were
imagined scenes that had never happened but could have and,
somehow, did.

No, this time it was like watching B-roll from a horror movie.
It was centipedes and cockroaches, spiders and snakes, scorpions
crawling over skeletons, and gigantic worms coming out of human
orifices. It was the worst of the worst of my mind's shadow, and
I lay there peacefully—reverently, even—and watched it all
unfold. And that's when I heard the voice.

Nothing is scary.

I didn't know whose voice it was: mine? God's? That of some
other celestial being? Some combination of all of those things?
But it didn't matter; I wasn't wondering that at all. I was mesmer-
ized, captivated by the truth of the statement. *Nothing is scary.* I
knew, without having to consciously think it, that this message
didn't undermine my feeling scared; I knew feeling scared was
okay. Feeling scared was human, and being human was good.

I did feel scared of what had happened, was happening, and
might yet happen to my body, to my life. But even still, as I faced the
darkness of the unknown and stared into an uncertainty I had never
imagined for myself, the words made sense to me. The universe
was a benevolent place; its creator a Thing of love. The worst of

the worst was here—who knew, perhaps the end was here—and everything was good. Everything held. Nothing was scary.

Questions for Prayer and Reflection

1. What has your relationship to horror and gore been like throughout your life, in either the secular or the spiritual realm? Has it evolved?

2. Have you yet looked at your own death without turning away in fear? How do you prepare yourself for such a thing?

3. (If you aren't familiar with the term *spiritual bypassing,* take a moment to look it up.) How has spiritual bypassing played a part in the way you work through things like trauma and fear? Have you yet stepped into a more mature faith that is able to hold such uncomfortable things without turning away?

Rest in peace.
In me
the meaning of your lives
is still
unfolding.

—ALICE WALKER

Acknowledgments

THANK YOU TO the team at Convergent and Penguin Random House for seeing the vision for this book and jumping on board to put it out into the world. A massive thanks in particular to my editor, Matt Burdette, who has made me feel heard and valued since day one and whose trustworthy eye so reliably sees what mine misses.

Keely Boeving, being able to depend on an agent as committed and personal as you takes enormous weight off my shoulders and frees me to do my part well. Thank you.

I am grateful for my writer friends who make this potentially lonely profession one of relationship and love instead. Camcron Bellm, your companionship is a breath of fresh air. Laura Fanucci, Stina Kielsmeier-Cook, and Ellie Roscher, days spent writing at the cabin with you are some of my favorite days. Eric Clayton, I trusted you with the most tender chapter of this book and you held it with care. I am also indebted to my local friends, who refuse to leave me to my own "introverted writer" devices but lure me out of the house for coffee or whiskey or deep conversations.

Thank you to my colleagues at the National Catholic Reporter, through whom I have learned much—not only about writing, but about telling the right story. A special thank-you to Heidi Schlumpf, who took a chance on me as an editor. Thank you, too, to all the writers I get the privilege of editing. Working with you makes me a better writer myself.

I am deeply grateful to my family, extended and immediate, for the way they relentlessly support my writing. Eric, thank you for being genuinely proud of the work I do. I feel it.

Last but not least, thank you to all the women who read *Rewilding Motherhood* and *Feminist Prayers for My Daughter* and reflected back to me what I had a hunch to be true: that women are hungry to tell our own stories. I hope you feel I did justice to the women telling their own stories in this book. I hope they compel you to tell yours, too.

Bibliography

MUCH HAS BEEN written by and about the six women in this book, all of which can be used to help us understand both the lives of these mystics and the way those lives have been twisted to advance various ideological and theological agendas. Every translator and biographer is human; each will bring their own biases to the work, no matter how hard they might try to remain neutral. Acknowledging this reality helped me read with both an open mind and a critical eye and motivated me to find a variety of voices to illuminate each mystic, in hopes that the cacophony of perspectives might paint a fuller, truer picture of the women I admire. I encourage anyone curious to do the same.

That being said, I suspect it might be helpful to my readers for me to disclose the resources I personally preferred along the way. This list is not exhaustive, but it is yours for the taking.

The Life of Saint Teresa of Ávila by Herself by Teresa of Ávila, translated by J. M. Cohen (Penguin Classics)
The Interior Castle by St. Teresa of Avila, translation and introduction by Mirabai Starr (Riverhead Books)
The Book of Margery Kempe by Margery Kempe, Translation and Introduction by B. A. Windeatt (Penguin Classics)

Scivias by Hildegard of Bingen, Translated by Mother
   Columba Hart and Jane Bishop (Paulist Press)
Hildegard of Bingen: Devotions, Prayers, & Living Wisdom,
   Edited by Mirabai Starr
Revelation of Love by Julian of Norwich, Translated by John
   Skinner (Image Books)
The Showings of Julian of Norwich: A New Translation,
   Translated by Mirabai Starr (Hampton Roads Publishing)
Story of a Soul: The Autobiography of St. Thérèse of Lisieux,
   Translated from the Original Manuscripts by John Clarke,
   OCD (ICS Publications)
Catherine of Siena: The Dialogue, by Catherine of Siena,
   Introduction and Translation by Suzanne Noffke (Paulist
   Press)
Catherine of Siena, by Sigrid Undset (Ignatius Press)

ABOUT THE AUTHOR

SHANNON K. EVANS is the spirituality and culture editor for the *National Catholic Reporter*. She is the author of *Feminist Prayers for My Daughter* and *Rewilding Motherhood*. She and her family make their home in Iowa.

SHANNONKEVANS.COM

ABOUT THE ARTIST

DANI is a writer and illustrator from Costa Rica. Her blog and store, And Her Saints, aim to illustrate the Holy and the Divine in ways that affirm and represent those at the margins of society. Their work has been featured in *U.S. Catholic* and *Beloved: A Butch-Femme Zine*.